THE polka king

the life of FRANKIE YANKOVIC

as told to

ROBERT DOLGAN

DILLON/LIEDERBACH, INC.
CLEVELAND

THE POLKA KING: THE LIFE OF FRANKIE YANKOVIC
AS TOLD TO ROBERT DOLGAN

PUBLISHED BY:
DILLON/LIEDERBACH, INC.
14591 MADISON AVENUE • CLEVELAND, OHIO 44107

Library of Congress Catalog Card Number: 77-72539

International Standard Book Number: 0-913228-23-0

Manufactured in the United States of America

TYPOGRAPHY:
IDEAL TYPESETTING, INC.
5241 WEST 161st STREET • CLEVELAND, OHIO 44142

CONTENTS

Chapter		Page
I.	Yankovic Speaks	1
II.	Boyhood	15
III.	Cheesebox	30
IV.	The Start	39
V.	June	50
VI.	War	63
VII.	Just Because	75
VIII.	Johnny Pecon	83
IX.	Long, Long Trail	101
X.	Breakup	132
XI.	Boys Will Be Boys	140
XII.	Family's Reply	150
XIII.	Pat	168
XIV.	Financial Bombs	177
XV.	The Show Goes On	186
XVI.	Polka People's Comments	210

ACKNOWLEDGMENTS

Hans Ammelounx, Martin (Heinie Martin) Antoncic, Eddie Arenz, Bob Bandy, Kenny Bass, Marion Belle, Ann Birsa, Denny Boneck, Lee Bower, Ed Bucar, Bruce Burger, Bill Bykowski, Tops Cardone, Ed Chay, Bobby Chick, Roger DiBenedict, Rose Drenik, Tony Drenik, Bill Dunlavey, Will Gliha, Laura Glozr, Buddy Griebel, Richard Gygli, Ed Grosel, Sherry Haaker, Eddie Habat, John Habat, John Hokavar, Al Jalen, Jean Jelenc, John Kausek, Eddie Kenik, John (Cookie) Kolovich, Dick Kossins, Jim Kozel, Grant Kozera, Patsy Krall, Herman Kravos, Mary Kravos, Marty (King) Kukovich, Joe Kumel, Frank J. Lausche, Lud Leskovar, Al Leslie, Joe Luzar, Norm Marggraff, Al Markic, Jimmy Maupin, Justine Mervar, Tom Milakovic, Josephine Misic, Joey Miskulin, Al Naglitch, Frank Novak, Ken Novak, Lee Novak, Jack O'Breza, Jr., Walter Ostanek, Carl Paradiso, Doc Perko, Frank Perme, Tony Petkovsek, Joe Plesivec, John Rebernisek, Carl Rohwetter, John Sandison, Bill Savatski, Bill Seles, Joe Siedlik, John Simcic, Sr., Steve Simcic, Ron Sluga, Don Sosnoski, Ray Smolik, Dick Sodja, Herman Spero, Frank Spilar, Anne Spiller, Bill Srnick, Eddy Stampfl, Ruthe Stampfl, Frank Sterle, Ray Strumbly, Al Tratnik, Lou Trebar, Joe Trolli, Richie Vadnal, Zarko Valencic, John Wagner, Lawrence Welk, Jeff Winard, Joe White, Judy Wilcox, Paul Wilcox, Andrea Yankovic (McKinnie), Frank Yankovic, Jr., Jerry Yankovic, John Yankovic, June Yankovic, Linda Yankovic (Konrad), Mark Yankovic, Pat Yankovic, Richard Yankovic, Robert Yankovic, and Mary Ziegenhorn.

Special thanks to Cecilia Dolgan, who helped with the interviewing and typed the manuscript.

This Book is Dedicated to All the People Who Like to Listen to Frankie Yankovic's Music

CHAPTER I

YANKOVIC SPEAKS

I guess I've slowed up a little. In my heyday, from the late 1940s through the middle 1960s, me and the boys in the band played as many as three hundred one-nighters a year. We would travel about 100,000 miles a year by car and we'd get home for maybe twenty-five days out of that whole time.

For a fellow who had a wife and eight children, as I did in those days, that was a pretty rough way to make a living. It was a life I wouldn't recommend to anybody, but it was the best life for me.

Today I'm still at it, 45 years after it all began. I've cut down some, but I'm still playing my accordion about 200 nights a year all over the United States. And when the spirit moves me I play in places like Germany, Hawaii, Spain and Yugoslavia. In 1975, for the first time, I even went to Alaska, where I'm pleased to say we played to standing-room-only audiences in Fairbanks and Anchorage.

I wouldn't be surprised if I travel more than any other 61-year-old man in America. Heck, maybe I travel more than any man in America, period.

Just to give you a typical example, let me tell you about a jaunt me and the Yanks took recently. In the space of one month we performed in Petoskey, Michigan; Oshkosh, Wisconsin; Peoria, Illinois; Raton, New Mexico; Lafayette, Colorado; Denver, Colorado; Leadville, Colorado; Pueblo, Colorado; Albuquerque, New Mexico; Phoenix, Arizona; El Paso, Texas; Waukegan, Illinois; Sturdevant, Wisconsin; St. Louis, Missouri, and Sherman, Illinois.

After playing sixteen cities in thirty days, I returned to my home in Cleveland. But my vacation didn't last long. Four days later I was on the move again, starting with consecutive one-nighters in Cheboygan, Michigan; Milwaukee, Wisconsin, and Joliet, Illinois.

That kind of schedule repeats itself month after month, although lately I've been trying to stay home at least four nights a week.

What can I do? The people still want me. I could have more jobs now than I ever did. But I promised my second wife, Pat, who is thirty years younger than me, that I would try to stay home more.

In fact, I've told Pat that when I'm 65 I'm going to cut down to one or two dances a week. I mean it when I say that, but Pat doubts that it will ever happen. She says I'd wither away if I ever got off the stage.

I guess that deep down I know she's right. I was bitten by the stage bug early and I never got over the infection. It cost me my first wife and family, but I know I'll always be a slave to it. Life is never sweeter to me than when I'm playing a rousing polka and making people happy.

There's another big reason I stay on the road as much as I do—the many good friends I've made all over the country. If I was like other traveling musicians, I would have quit long ago.

Most musicians play a job and go back to some dingy dressing room between sets. When the night ends, they go to a lonely motel room and play cards or watch television.

They're always strangers on the road, playing for people they don't know and don't care about.

With me and the boys in the band, it's different. Our work is more personal. I have close friends wherever I go and every night on the road is like New Year's Eve. I've been a godfather and best man for so many people. I've lost count. Most of the time we don't even stay in motels. My friends make us stay in their homes. They'd be insulted if we didn't.

We don't just play a job, take the money and get out. It's always like a big reunion. I've been coming back to most of the towns we play in for thirty years, so naturally people come to the bandstand and reminisce.

They ask me if I remember the song I played for them the night they got engaged, or they ask if I recall the great time we had that New Year's Eve in 1951. Usually I do. I always did have a good memory.

People buy our records right off the bandstand while we're playing and every once in a while we run into some jolly soul who wants to come up and play an instrument with the band.

If the guy's not drunk, I always let him come up and play. It makes for a better show and a lot of fun. Besides, sometimes you find a musician who's really talented. That's exactly how I latched on to Joey Miskulin, one of the finest accordion players anywhere. Joey played with us the first time when he was thirteen, beginning a friendship that has lasted ever since.

I especially like to give young boys a break. And if a kid suddenly gets stage fright and freezes, I'll take the lead on my accordion and try to make him look good. Sometimes, if I let a local kid play too much, though, people will give me hell. They'll tell me they came to hear me, not somebody else. I only tell you this to emphasize the down-home attitude our audiences have toward us.

Another thing I never do is turn down a request for a song. I figure I'm there to play what the people want, not what I want. Above all, I'm not there to play songs that will give me a chance to show off. I've seen guys who play songs just because they're hard to play. They want to show the crowd how good they are, even if the song stinks. I'm not like that. If somebody wants me to play "The Clairene Waltz" for his birthday, or "I've Got a Date with Molly," for an anniversary, I'm always happy to oblige.

In the same way, I always answer every letter I get. It was like that even in the old days, when I'd get maybe one hundred letters a week. I figure if somebody takes the trouble to sit down and write to me, then I should have the courtesy to write back. I guess it's just the way I was raised.

You can see why I continue working. It's pure fun. If I am the most traveled 61-year-old man in America, I may also be having more fun than any 61-year-old in America.

I know there are a lot of people who laugh at the polka and call it white-socks music, but that doesn't bother me. I've heard that kind of stuff all my life. It comes mostly from people who are afraid to admit they get a kick out of the polka for fear they'll be thought of as unsophisticated.

But I've never yet played for a crowd that didn't like our music. I don't care where it was—at a ball for the governor of Ohio, in a Las Vegas motel, or at a fancy night club like the Mocambo on the Sunset Strip in Hollywood.

The people might have come in there with their noses in the air, but they stayed to clap and dance and sing. And if they walked out saying they had a good time, but that they really think the polka is for peasants, well, that's okay too. They don't fool me any. If they want to kid themselves, let them. Sophisticated people have always had trouble expressing themselves anyway.

Although there are an increasing number of people such as doctors, lawyers and architects in our audiences, I like to think of myself as the blue collar worker's musician. I'm proud of that. After all, this country was built on the blood and sweat and guts of the blue collar man.

I'm a blue collar guy and so was my father. So were most of the people I've been close to. I'm just an average guy who is lucky enough to understand what a lot of average guys in the country like to hear.

Many a time I've gone into a little village whose downtown consisted of a barbershop and a grocery store. Sometimes one of my new musicians says, "What the heck are we doing in a town like this? Nobody even lives here. We won't have any crowd at the dance tonight."

But I always say, "Don't worry. Wait until tonight. Then talk. We'll have a good crowd, I guarantee you." And we do. People flock in from as far as 200 miles away.

Johnny Carson talked about that when I was on his television show. Johnny told the network audience that he remembered the days when me and the Yanks would come into his little hometown of Norfolk, Nebraska. He said that our arrival was always the biggest event of the year there. Johnny called me the biggest man in the history of polka music.

I appreciated the compliment, but it was like saying that Babe Ruth was a baseball player, or that Picasso could paint.

It is obvious. I hate to brag, but nobody else in the polka world has come even close to doing what I've done.

For instance, I've made two polka records that were million-sellers, "Just Because," and "The Blue Skirt Waltz." That's something that no other American polka musician has ever done.

To put it in perspective, a polka album that sells 5,000 copies today is considered a healthy hit. A copy of "Just Because," in fact, is in the Library of Congress in Washington, D. C., as a permanent piece of Americana.

Sure, there have been other polka records that sold a million copies. The Andrews Sisters had "The Beer Barrel Polka," Arthur Godfrey clicked with "She's Too Fat for Me," and Bobby Vinton did it in 1975 with "My Melody of Love."

But those were records sung by people who were famous in the field of popular music. They sang to an audience of maybe 50 million people and had the full power and money of the big-time entertainment centers promoting them. The polka audience is much smaller. The only other polka musician to make a gold record was Frank Wojnarowski of Connecticut, who did it with a Polish song, "My Mama," about ten years ago.

While I'm patting myself on the back, I might as well tell you I've had some pretty good paydays. In my biggest year, 1950, I grossed about $250,000, and cleared $80,000. That was a lot of scratch in those pre-inflationary days. A friend once gave me a $2,000 tip for entertaining at a private party.

I don't make as much money as I used to, but I still collect plenty of royalties. But I'm not kidding myself about that. If I'd stop traveling and promoting my records, my royalties would go down to nothing fast.

I've recorded about thirty albums with Columbia and RCA Victor and I don't know how many singles. I've sold six million records. I've played the biggest and smallest night clubs in virtually every town in the land, and I've received so many awards and plaques from civic organizations that I'm running out of wall space. Just the other day, when we played at the Gottscheer Hall in Ridgewood, N. Y., I was honored by a plaque and resolution from the New York State Assembly.

Further, I am the only polka musician to perform consistently on network TV. I've been on with Carson twice and also with people such as Arthur Godfrey, David Frost, Lawrence Welk, Phil Donahue, Kate Smith, and Patti Page. I even had my own weekly television show at different times in Cleveland (WEWS), Chicago (WGN), and Buffalo (WKBK). And I still appear almost every week on WEWS' Polka Varieties TV show, which has been running for twenty years.

Asked to comment on my career, my good friend Lawrence Welk said, "As a polka enthusiast of long standing, I've been a Frankie Yankovic fan from his earliest days in the business. I've always admired his natural instinct for the proper 'feel' of a polka. He has a knack for setting the perfect tempo for each selection. It's impossible to overestimate his invaluable contribution to our musical culture. His famous record of 'Just Because' is still a classic and one of my all-time favorites. In addition, Frankie possesses all the qualities which are the mark of a warm and wonderful human being."

Tony Petkovsek, one of Cleveland's most influential polka disc jockies, summed up my career this way: "There has never been anyone like Yankovic around the polka scene before, and there probably never will be anybody like him again. He is the greatest promoter the polka has ever had and is the most copied entertainer in the history of polka music. His records have even been bootlegged. People tape his music from television, radio or records and then put it out as their own record."

Eddie Habat, the fine Cleveland accordionist, calls me "The Pathfinder." He points out that I brought the polka into areas of America where they'd seldom heard of them. I went into a lot of towns that didn't even have an accordion player, and those same towns now have their own polka bands.

My name is recognized even by people who don't care at all about polka music. Petkovsek likes to tell a story about some black people who patronized a bar his father owned in a Cleveland factory district.

These black fellows would come into the bar after work and when one of my records was on the juke box they'd say, "Man, that sounds like Frankie Yankowitz." They may not have pronounced it right, but they knew my name.

Sure there have been a lot of outstanding polka bands

through the years. I don't want to start naming them, because I'm sure to leave somebody out and that'll cause hard feelings. But there are dozens and dozens of them who played terrific music.

And yet, these fellows, good as they were, were practically unknown outside their immediate territories. Wojnarowski, for example, confines most of his playing to the East Coast. Cleveland's Johnny Pecon was a brilliant accordionist, but who ever heard of him in Las Vegas or San Francisco? The same goes for the others.

This is true, of course, not necessarily because I was a better accordion player than they were, but because they didn't make the commitment that I did.

Most of the time, I supported myself and my family with my music, nothing else. I've lived on the road for forty years. Not many people can do that. It takes a lot of stomach. Everybody wants to stay home where life is cozy and mama will bring you a bowl of hot soup if you're sick. But that's one thing that even my critics will admit—I always had nerve.

For most polka players, music is only a sideline. They have other jobs and don't depend on polkas for their livelihood.

Pecon, for example, was the custodian at Cleveland's City Hall. Richie Vadnal of Cleveland is a fireman. Roman Possedi of Chicago is a railroad engineer, and Jack Tady of Pittsburgh is a schoolteacher.

Obviously, these fellows couldn't, or didn't want to, compete with me in nationwide appeal. While I'm traveling the country, their jobs keep them close to home and hearth.

What's more, I don't gear my music toward any particular ethnic group. For instance, a fellow like Li'l Wally Jagiello plays mostly Polish music, while fellows like Al Markic and Jake Zagger play strictly Slovenian.

I always figured that if I aimed my music toward only one nationality, I would be cutting down my market. So I tried to develop a sound that all nationalities could identify with.

That's why I'm proud of the fact that in 1969 the International Polka Association, which is primarily a Polish organization, made me, a Slovenian, and Li'l Wally the first men inducted into the Polka Hall of Fame in Chicago.

I'm also proud that I hold the title of America's Polka King. The first time I won that laurel was in the Milwaukee Auditorium in 1948, in a contest promoted by the major record companies. Each one had their top band represented.

Those who competed were Sammy Madden, Louis Bashell, Lawrence Duchow and his Red Ravens, the Six Fat Dutchmen, led by tuba-thumping Harold Loeffelmacher, and yours truly and all the Yanks.

There were 8,000 spectators at the contest. Each one got a ballot to vote on, and each band played for a half hour. All the bands were keyed up and really wanted to win.

I think I was near the peak of my career then, with one of my best bands. I had Pecon with me, Georgie Cook on the banjo, Whitey Lovsin on drums, Church Srnick on bass and Al Naglitch on the piano. We were all Cleveland boys who had known each other for years.

The Milwaukee Journal, which covered the event, reported that when we took the bandstand we looked as relaxed as sleeping babies. There was a reason for that. We were well fortified with anti-freeze, if you know what I mean. Me and the Yanks had stopped at our Milwaukee headquarters, Rebernisek's Bar, before the contest. The bar was packed with well-wishers and we really got primed for the competition. The boys were all good mixers and loved to have good times.

When we started to play in the auditorium that night the crowd came close around the stage, as though it was a bar-room songfest. We had a lot of friends there, good followers of our music. We started off with a song called "The Three Yanks Polka," named after my first three children.

I took the melody, with Pecon improvising runs between the notes. The rhythm section was cracking. The whiskey was running. The crowd went crazy and the rest was easy.

When we finished "The Three Yanks," the crowd insisted we play it again. We had to do it three times, with the crowd singing and clapping along. Then we followed with our big hit, "Just Because." We had a hard time getting off the stage. When they counted the votes we outpolled the next band by 8 to 1.

I know there's been talk that me and the Yanks went into

the crowd that night and did some politicking, talking people into voting for us. I've even heard that I grabbed hundreds of ballots and wrote my name in on them myself.

Take it from me, that's all baloney. It was a legitimate contest. All we got out of winning was a big cup, but that's something I wouldn't sell for any money. We took it back to Rebernisek's after the contest, filled it with champagne, and had more fun.

We also won the polka king contest the next two years, after which the competition ended. The major record companies weren't interested in sponsoring the contests anymore because there were too many independent record makers getting into the act. I can understand that. It would be foolish for a company like Columbia, for example, to take a chance on having its house band beat out by some unknown group.

The polka king title doesn't really mean that much anymore because there haven't been any official contests since we won. But I still take it seriously. I have "America's Polka King" engraved on my stationery and it's written in big letters on the mobile home I travel in.

I'm jealous of the title to the point where I sued a newspaperman, who I felt had inferred that Johnny Pecon was the polka champion in a story he wrote in his paper in 1968.

I wasn't really mad at the man. He is a nice guy and usually a good writer. But he was a Johnny-come-lately in the polka world and there was a lot of things in it he wouldn't know about yet.

He made it sound in his story that Pecon was the biggest man in polka history. He said he got the polka barrel rolling in this country.

The story bothered me, but I didn't do anything about it. Then one day I chanced meeting the author at the YMCA. We were both taking a workout and a sauna bath, and we were introduced. I took that opportunity to fill him in. I told him it was fine that he wrote a nice story about Pecon, but I said I thought that he had made some mistakes.

After I told him the full story, I asked for a retraction of the article. He said he would do better than that and that he would write another front page story, clarifying the situation and giving me the credit I was entitled to. But time went on and the story never came out.

So I got mad and sued him and the papers for one million dollars. Eventually I dropped the case. The lawyers' fees and red tape just weren't worth it. I didn't care about the money anyway. I just wanted the retraction.

That was one of the few times I ever stuck up for my rights. For years I let people take shots at me. I just laughed them off, figuring that it was human nature. People are always going to knock you if you're successful. It's plain jealousy. They'll help you on the way up, but they'll turn on you if you get too big.

But lately I figure I deserve to answer my detractors. I've been humble long enough. I spent my life in this business, hurting nobody, keeping quiet through all the stories and rumors.

Now I figure it's my turn to tell the truth about all the controversial things that have happened. That's one reason for this book.

What hurts most is that 99 per cent of the criticism against me comes from people in my hometown of Cleveland, Ohio. You know the old saying—familiarity breeds contempt. A lot of the knocks come from the musicians.

Do you know, for example, that I've never been invited to join the Cleveland Polkats Club? If that's not ironic, I don't know what is. I don't want to sound petty and it's not really important, but it's just symbolic of the way a lot of Cleveland musicians treat me.

Virtually every polka musician in town is in that club. It's a social thing. A lot of them have played with my band at one time or another. In a way, I'm the godfather of them all. I know I'm on the road a lot, but they could have at least asked me to become an honorary member.

Some musicians have been rapping me for years. They can't get at me any other way, so they make remarks of a personal nature. They mock the way I talk and sing, with my Slovene accent, and they say I'm a mediocre accordionist.

When Pecon left me, they said I was through. When Tops Cardone left me, they said I was through. They said the same thing when Joey Miskulin and Joe Sekardi left. They said I was a nobody, a faker. They said it wasn't Yankovic who put the music across, but his side men.

I always gave my side men credit. It's a lot like a ball team. You have to play together. Without them, I'd be nothing. But by now I think I've proved my critics were all wrong.

I'm still going strong, 28 years after Pecon and I split and I've had hundreds of side men. If I wasn't doing something right the people would have wised up to me long ago.

When it comes to accordion playing, I won't take a back seat to anybody. Maybe I don't play as well as some of the real virtuosos, like Myron Floren or Miskulin, but then I'm pretty good with a song and I have a certain onstage style. I play from the heart.

That's what people like in this field anyway. They're not going to worry if you hit a clinker or two.

But I still see the jealous looks and I hear the knocks, always behind my back. I tried to answer them when I went on the radio recently with Cleveland disc jockey Bruce Burger. Bruce is one of the few polka deejays who isn't afraid to get involved in controversy, and he conducted a talk show with me. I wanted to clear the air, so I invited people to call in and make their charges against me, without giving their names. Nobody would do it, but I still hear the whispers.

It isn't all bad, of course. One of my all-time thrills came when the prestigious Federation of Slovenian Homes in Cleveland honored me as its man of the year at a beautiful banquet. The Slovenian National Home was packed with about 1,000 people and they broke into impromptu song as Cecilia Dolgan sang some of my big tunes. It felt great to finally be recognized by the people who knew me from the start. A lot of good friends also came from as far as St. Louis, Denver and Milwaukee.

But through the whole affair, I couldn't help remembering that the first testimonial ever held for me was in Pittsburgh, and not in my hometown. Marty King put together that Pittsburgh fete in my behalf and he even remarked about it. He said, "Son of a bitch, Frank, they should have had this for you first in Cleveland. You had to come all this way."

In fact, six other Cleveland Slovenes were picked as men of the year before they got around to me. I was beginning to think I was forgotten. But maybe I was wrong in feeling ignored. After all, Frank Lausche wasn't honored until the year before me, and Lausche is by far the most important Slovenian in the history of the United States, and a native Clevelander to boot. Lausche was elected governor of Ohio five times, was mayor of Cleveland twice, and was a U.S. Senator twice. And yet, five Cleveland Slovenes were honored as men of the year before he was.

I'm often asked, by the way, to name the best polka accordionists. In my opinion, the best two Americans I've heard are Pecon and Miskulin. Joey doesn't think he's as good as the late Pecon, but he's wrong.

But the top man I've ever heard anywhere is Slavko Avsenik, the great Slovenian who lives in Yugoslavia. Nobody I ever heard can touch him, without a doubt. He's played concerts in Europe before 80,000 people and has sold millions of records there. A terrific showman and an even better composer, Avsenik is my own private polka king.

When Avsenik was in Cleveland several years ago, he had dinner at my restaurant. I was enthused to have him there and did everything I could to please him and his musicians. It was the first time I had ever met him. But he just sat there and was really cold. I was disappointed. I couldn't understand it.

Finally, I asked his manager why he didn't want to talk to me. "He's mad at you for that song you and Johnny Pecon stole from him," the manager said.

I straightened out Avsenik immediately. I told him that Pecon had made that record, not me. Johnny had recorded one of Avsenik's incomparable melodies with English words put to it. The result was a song called "Little Fella." I had nothing to do with it. Avsenik was under the impression that Pecon and I were still in the same band, as we had been years before. After Avsenik understood, we became the best of friends.

Lojze Slak, another Yugoslavian recording star, is often mentioned in the same breath with Avsenik. But to be honest with you, Slak can't even begin to compare with Avsenik as an international showman. Avsenik appeals to everybody, while Slak's audience is strictly Slovenian. You can't give Slak any modern music, because he doesn't play it.

Slak favors playing only the button box. That's an extremely limited instrument. Playing it is comparable to playing the piano without using the black keys. There are a lot of songs. you can't do on it. I should know, I learned to play on the button box.

Don't get me wrong, Slak is a good musician and composer, but if you take away his vocalists he doesn't have much of a show. There are any number of American button box men, Frank Novak and Joe Kusar, for instance, who play just as well as he does, if not better.

It's a funny thing about Slak. He's an entirely different guy than he was the first time I met him. When he came to the U.S. in 1970, I was introduced to him at the Slovenian National Home in Cleveland, where he was appearing.

He put his arms around me and told me that I had always been his idol. He said he listened to my records in Yugoslavia. The next year, when we went to Europe, I stayed at his house and we had a lot of fun.

But when he came back to Cleveland in 1975 he had changed. I went to see him at the Front Row Theater, where he was rehearsing for a show that night. We shook hands, but I could tell right away that there was something wrong. He was cold. I don't know if he got a big head or what.

I was really embarrassed, because I had some friends from Chicago with me. They wanted to take a picture of me with him, and he said, "Later, after the rehearsal." He brushed us off, and we had to wait around to get the picture. I didn't even want it, but I knew my friends did. Otherwise I would have walked out.

The whole episode really burned me up. I couldn't help thinking that Slak wouldn't even have been playing in Cleveland if I hadn't started the polka craze years before. I blame our own people for building him up the way they did. They pay him good money to come to America, and they treat him like a visiting emperor when he arrives. No wonder he thinks he's something special.

But enough of that. Let's get on with it. It's been a great life, full of triumphs, disappointments and action. It all began on July 28, 1915, when I was born in Davis, West Virginia.

CHAPTER II

BOYHOOD

My people come from the little republic of Slovenia, in what is now Yugoslavia. The Slovenes are a generally unknown people, probably because of their lack of population. There are only 1.8 million of them in the world. As I travel America, people are always asking me, "What's a Slovenian?" They often confuse us with Slovaks, who are an entirely different group. They never heard of us.

But the Slovenes are and have been an intelligent, civilized race. They print more books per capita than any other nation in Europe, they have one of the highest literacy rates in the world, and they control the commerce of Yugoslavia in a manner far out of proportion with their numbers.

The distinguished historian William Shirer, who wrote "The Rise and Fall of the Third Reich," once paid a marvelous compliment to Slovenia's capital city, Ljubljana.

"Here is a city for the whole world to emulate," Shirer wrote. "Its streets and parks are filled with statues of writers and thinkers, but not one military man has been so honored." Ljubljana, by the way, translates into Loveland, which may tell you more about the Slovenes than anything else.

My father, Andy, was born in Kal, Slovenia, in 1879, while my mother, Rose Mele, was born in Cerknica, Slovenia, in 1886. Neither knew each other in the old country. They both came to America around 1903, and both came alone. My mother was only 17 at the time. Think about that a little—a 17-year-old girl coming alone to a new country, frightened and apprehensive, and not even knowing the language. But that was the way things were then. A lot of immigrants were even younger, 13 or 14. All they had to bolster them was a picture of their mother in their cheap suitcases.

My mother lived in New York for a while, working as a maid. Then she heard that kitchen help was needed in a lumber camp in Davis, West Virginia, where a lot of Slovenes were working.

She met my dad at the camp. He was employed there as a blacksmith and was sending money back to Slovenia to help support his parents. My dad continued to do that as long as his parents were alive. A lot of people did that in those days. Life was so much better financially in America.

Anyway, my dad and mother got married in 1910 and it wasn't long before they were running the camp. My mother was in charge of feeding the 76 men who worked there, while my father was the foreman.

My mother and her kitchen helpers made three meals a day for the lumberjacks. Every morning they packed 76 lunch pails and made dozens of loaves of bread, using about 100 pounds of flour daily.

The camp was like a small company town. The lumberjacks, most of them Slovene bachelors, would sleep and eat there, and every month the company would take money out of their checks and pay my parents for the room and board.

In the meantime, my dad was also doing a healthy business in bootlegging, selling wine and whiskey to the men.

I don't know how they had the time to do it, but my father and mother also raised a family. They had three daughters, Josephine, Rose and Mary, before I finally came along in 1915. We were all born at the lumber camp.

But my father was gone by the time I was born. No, he didn't desert the family. He just had to beat a strategic retreat.

You see, the local authorities heard about my dad's bootlegging and arrested him. A trial date was set up, but the boss of the company town advised my dad to get out of camp. He told him if he stayed he'd be sure to get a stiff fine or even a jail sentence. West Virginia was a dry state.

So my dad tearfully kissed his little family goodbye, scooped up all the money, and high-tailed it for Cleveland, the center of Slovene life in America. My mother couldn't go with him because she was expecting me at any moment.

I was born a few days later and then my mother brought me and my three sisters to Cleveland by train to join dad. I was only eight days old.

I hope the Davis police won't come after me to collect my dad's fine now that they know where to find me.

Our first home in Cleveland was at 15702 Saranac Road, in the Slovene-Italian section of Collinwood. It was like living in Europe. Hardly anybody talked English. Saranac, by the way, was later known as Raisinjack Alley because of all the bootleggers operating there.

It was a lively neighborhood, but there was no problem on the streets. Anyone could walk them without fear. The little street trouble that existed usually arose from fights between young men over girls.

The saloons were the center of social life for the young men. Women weren't allowed inside but otherwise the taverns were friendly places, offering free lunches of salami and hard-boiled eggs for a nickel beer.

The young Slovene workingman usually liked his whiskey, and it came in handy during the awful influenza epidemic of 1918, when 3,000 Clevelanders died. My father was going to so many funerals that he was afraid he'd get sick too. He went to a doctor who prescribed a pint of whiskey a day. Many an old-timer will swear today that he stayed alive only because he was smart enough to keep his body in a state of constant inebriation.

My mother had her own way of protecting us kids from the flu. She would hang garlic in little bags around our necks and soak our handkerchiefs in camphorated oil.

The funerals were something, big productions. When an important person or a child died, the whole neighborhood would turn out. Streetcars draped in black would carry the deceased to the cemetery and a lot of times a brass band would lead the procession.

The brass bands were also important to the Slovenian lodge parades, which were held almost every Sunday during warm weather. Kids would sit proudly on the curbs to watch their fathers in their navy blue lodge uniforms, marching sternly to the music. They knew how to run parades in those days. You didn't see any cars diluting them. Everybody walked.

When my dad first came into Collinwood, he worked as a crane operator for M. Cohen & Son, a scrap dealer on the corner of East 165th Street and St. Clair Avenue. That outfit later became Viking Steel Co. When I was four or five, I'd take his lunch to him every day.

After a while, my dad went into partnership with Anton Nemec, and they bought a hardware store at 16131 St. Clair. It was called New Center Hardware.

In addition, my parents always added to their income by having boarders. It was a common thing then. We always had about seven or eight Slovene bachelors living in the house. They paid $25 a month for a bed and three meals a day.

Our life centered around these boarders. Men like Max Zelodec, Joe Dolgan and Louie Mankush were like part of the family. In fact, two of my sisters later married boarders. Rose married Tony Drenik and Mary wed Herman Kravos.

When we lived on Saranac we had only four rooms so we kids had to sleep in the living room. When I was real small, I would sleep with two of my sisters on the sofa, while Mary, who had a leg ailment, had the luxury of sleeping alone on a three-quarter bed that folded up into the wall. Kids don't realize how easy they have it today.

The boarders would all sleep in one room, two or three to a a bed. They didn't care. They were young, jolly guys and they were just happy to be in America. When I got older, I moved into the boarders' room and slept with them.

When I was about eight, my folks moved into a bigger house in the same neighborhood, at 692 East 160th, at the corner of Midland Avenue. My dad had it built for $11,000. It was all brick, a real beauty for those days. The father of Milan Kapel, now a prominent Cleveland builder, liked it so much that he built one exactly like it on the next street.

We had a happy life, with a lot of people always around our home. I guess that's how I got used to crowds. Even today, I like to have plenty of company.

Us kids were all raised to help around the house. The girls would help my mother cook and clean, while my big chore was taking care of the balinca court my father had put in the yard.

For those of you who don't know, balinca is a first cousin of the English game of lawn bowling. The Italians call the same sport bocce. The game is always accompanied by fierce shouts and a lot of betting. It is probably the national game of the Slovenes, and is played in all the Slovene cultural halls in America. They even hold tournaments today.

Every morning, especially on Saturdays and Sundays, I would have to water our balinca court with a fine spray. Then I would have to get out the roller and go over every inch of the court, which was about 60 feet long and 12 feet wide. Believe me, that fine dirt court had to be manicured so that it was like a carpet or a bowling alley. The balls had to roll true.

People would come from all over the neighborhood and sit on our back porch to watch the games. Most of the boarders played, including my dad's brother, Uncle Joe, or Stric Joze.

My dad and his brother had terrific games. They were both warm-hearted extroverts and great rivals. When they played everybody would watch. Oh, how they swore and competed against each other. They'd fight for a penny. After dark, they would play cards. Many a time the cards were ripped up in anger.

My uncle Joe, by the way, lived in this country for 20 years. He got married in Europe, and had three daughters. Then he came here alone and worked for the New York Central Railroad. He always sent money home to his family. Finally, after 20 years, he retired from his job, got his pension, and went back to Slovenia. He died within a year.

While the balinca games were being contested, my mother and sisters would sell home-made wine, whiskey and beer to the players and spectators. The bowlers would play mostly for drinks, occasionally for a few dollars. They weren't really gamblers, but just played for the fun. I had to run around and pick up the bottles and glasses when the drinkers were finished with them.

It wasn't all work, of course. I got quite a few chances to practice balinca and got pretty good at it. I learned to hit the ball "skuz lufta," or "resta," through the air, in the old Slovene manner. I can still play pretty good today.

About a year ago at Holmes Avenue Slovenian Home, John

Frankie at age three.

Max Zelodec, the accordionist who first inspired and taught Yankovic: 1925.

Friends, relatives, and boarders behind the Yankovic homestead, 1928. Young Frank, leaning on the front fender, is standing next to his uncle Joe and his mother is directly behind them. His father, Andy, is seated on the running board. The man with the accordion is Joe Dolgan, the author's father.

Frank in his early teens — already playing for dances.

Frank and June slowly recovering from rented steeds.

The Yankovic Family in the late 1930s — front row (left to right): Mother Rose, sister Rose, father Andy; rear (left to right): sister Josephine, Frank, cousin Tony, and sister Mary.

Simcic challenged me to a game. John, a Cleveland tavern owner, is about the best balinca player in town. He thought I was going to be a fish. But I took a 20 to 15 lead and only needed one more point to win when he came up with six and nosed me out, 21 to 20. He hit my ball out resta for the six points.

Another time, when I was at the Italian Club in Pennsylvania, Marty King, my bass player, had me play the top player there. They thought I would be a sucker again, but I beat the guy by a pretty big score.

In Europe, when I visited my dad's hometown, I beat my cousin, a really good player. Nobody could get over it.

Balinca is my sport. I play golf too, but I can't get with it as well. It takes too long. I'm always thinking of the things I'm neglecting by spending a whole day on the links. I shoot about 92.

Getting back to my boyhood, our house was like a meeting place all the time. In the winters the boarders and others would play cards all night on weekends. They'd play Slovene games like Kenik Ruf or 66. They'd holler for wine and my mother would get out of bed and serve them. In the morning, she'd scrub the floor on her hands and knees. She was one of those practical, strong women who seemed to spend her whole life in the kitchen.

While dad sang and drank with the boarders, my mother would make money on the wine and pinch pennies. We had to have soup, potatoes and lettuce with every meal. *Tinstan krumpir* (home fries with onions) were my favorites. We had *polenta* (corn meal mush) for breakfast with coffee over it. We used to fight for the cream at the top of a bottle of milk.

We made a lot of our own food too. We'd cut up about four or five hogs each year and make our own ham and blood and rice sausages. And *mesene klobase.* I even learned how to skin the pig and cut the feet off. Then we'd take the meat and hang it on little sticks in the smoke house.

My dad had a Model T Ford and during the summer we'd go for long drives. Once we went all the way to Conneaut, 70 miles, to visit our cousins, the Sterles. It was a big trip in those days. Mom packed a basket of food. We talked about it for a week.

We'd also drive to Barberton or Madison or Geneva and buy *bezek* (berries) and grapes and plums to make whiskey. We'd also pick dandelions from a big empty lot on St. Clair and my dad would make dandelion wine out of them.

Those dandelions looked like weeds, but they also made a great salad if you knew how to handle them right. My mother would mix them with oil and vinegar and slice in some hard-boiled eggs. It was delicious. I still love dandelions to this day, although it's hard to find anybody making them anymore. People are rich today and dandelions aren't good enough for them. Believe me, they don't know what they're missing.

The boarders drank most of our wine. They liked the red wine best because the white was stronger and they couldn't drink as much of it.

I'd sit up with them until midnight, listening to them sing and argue about who came from the best village in Slovenia or who took too many steps and cheated in balinca. We all talked Slovenian in the house. I didn't learn English, in fact, until I went to school. There was no need to. You could get along just fine in our neighborhood talking nothing but Slovenian.

It was inevitable that my dad would get caught for bootlegging again. The federal agents came to our house and caught dad three times. He had to pay a fine of $115 each time.

For those of you who are too young to know, it was illegal to buy or sell whiskey in America from 1919 to 1933. Some do-gooders had convinced enough people that whiskey was going to ruin the country.

It was an idiotic law because it couldn't be enforced. It was ignored by almost everybody. Even though all the saloons were closed, people kept right on drinking in speakeasies and private homes. It was the era when bootlegging really flourished.

I'm not ashamed to admit dad was a bootlegger. Many of the fortunes of now-respected families in this country stand on the foundation of bootlegging.

My dad cooked his wine and whiskey in copper kettles and sometimes I stayed up all night watching him make it. I knew we were breaking the law, but I was intrigued by the cooking and processing and all that. I guess if it came right down to it, I could still remember how to cook a little whiskey today if I had to.

If the Feds came into the house, we kids were told by mom and dad to follow each one as they searched the house. We didn't trust them, because sometimes they would carry a bottle in with them and plant it in your closet, then use it for evidence against you.

There was another speakeasy across from my dad's hardware store. It was owned by my dad's best friend.

Whenever he would get a call every now and then that the Feds were on their way, he would roll his barrels of beer across St. Clair Avenue and hide them in the garage behind my dad's hardware store. We hid the whiskey under the floor. Sometimes us kids would sneak in there and drink the beer, mostly out of curiosity. It was the best beer.

I got into a few minor scrapes, but all in all I have to say I was a very good boy. I suppose I was a little spoiled because I was the only son, coming after three daughters. I was my mother's pet.

In the mornings, when she'd get me up to go to school, she'd pat me and talk to me in Slovenian like I was a baby. She'd call me "porkychek." I don't know why she called me that, except it had an affectionate sound to it.

She'd wash me and bundle me up to go to school. The girls, in the meantime, had to do everything for themselves. Sometimes, if I didn't like a meal too much, my mother would make me a special meal all for myself.

I learned to be a darn good cook just by watching my mother, and I loved to eat eggs. I'd eat about four every day. Anytime I was hungry I'd just go to the icebox and make some omelettes.

I continued to gorge myself on eggs until I was about nine, when I had my appendix removed. The doctor told us that my love of eggs had brought about the appendicitis. He warned it could bring on other illnesses and said I'd have to cut down. Naturally, we believed him.

When we lived on Saranac, there was another boy, Frank

Valencic, who lived upstairs. We called him Upstairs Frankie. I was Downstairs Frankie.

One day I got hold of the cigarets my mother always kept to sell to the boarders. There was a whole carton of them. Upstairs Frankie, in the meantime, stole some matches from his mother. We discovered the pleasures of cigaret smoking.

We would crawl underneath the porch and smoke, so nobody could see us, or we'd go into the basement into the empty wine barrels. One night mom smelled smoke and she came downstairs. She saw smoke coming out of the barrel and caught us.

Upstairs Frankie and Downstairs Frankie both got lickings from their fathers, who used straps. To this day, I have never had another cigaret.

When I was nine years old I startled everybody with a little escapade in my cousin Frank Spilar's car. Frank, who was only 16, had a beautiful 1924 Chevrolet. I watched him drive and pretty soon I knew how. The police of Cleveland were holding a picnic one Sunday, so I figured it would be a good time to drive the car. I figured there would be no police around.

I took the car and drove around the neighborhood by myself. I was so small that I could barely be seen over the steering wheel. When I got to East 159th Street and Holmes, I stopped and a car passed. It was a police car. The cops did a double take and saw this big black car with apparently nobody at the wheel.

When the police stopped the car, they were amazed to see me. Then they took me to the police station on Hayden and St. Clair and called dad, who came down and got me. Boy, was he mad. He started hitting me and yelling.

But mostly I just lived a boy's happy life. I liked to play dominoes and marbles and I was crazy about dogs. We had a beautiful cocker spaniel for years. I named him Clinker, after all the wrong notes I was hitting on the accordion. Years later I even recorded a song called the Clinker Polka.

But my big passion was the movies. Me and my cousin Frank Spilar, who had come to live with us from Indianapolis after his father died, would go to three or four shows a week. Mostly we went to the Five Points Theater, or the Plaza, which were both in the neighborhood. My favorite stars were Tom Mix, Buck Jones and Hoot Gibson, all cowboys, and Rin Tin Tin, the wonder dog.

When they'd show pictures of people traveling and leading glamorous lives, I'd say to Spilar, "Why can't we do things like that? Someday I'm going to." I was dreaming big things.

My mother would give us the 10 or 15 cents to go to the show and she'd say, "Don't tell dad where you got the money."

Sometimes dad would say, "Where were you all day, damn it."

But my dad liked me because I was, by and large, a very good boy. I worked hard at his hardware store after school and all day on Saturdays.

Hardware stores were different then and I learned a lot of trades there. If somebody needed a window pane I would put it in, and I learned how to make electrical repairs, cut pipes and sew leather. We did a lot of harness work, although there weren't too many horses left in Collinwood. I learned to wait on customers too.

Newlyweds would come in and give you a list of things for their whole house, from pots and pans to nails. It was strictly hardware—no appliances.

Whenever this one particular Italian woman would come in, dad would hide in the garage and make me wait on her. She would ask the price of this and that and I'd spend an hour bringing things off the top shelves, using a ladder. But she would never buy anything. She'd question everything. I can still see her face.

Occasionally, I was mischievous. When dad would leave the store for lunch, me and Spilar would take some bee-bees and a .22 rifle and I'd go into the basement and take a position by the window.

Spilar would stay upstairs by the door and when he'd see a girl walking alone, he'd yell down to me: "Hey, Yonkee, there's one coming now." (Spilar nicknamed me Yonkee in 1928.) Then I'd shoot the bee-bees at the girl's legs. She would look around and scratch them a bit and wonder what was going on. She couldn't see anything. It didn't hurt much, but it was sure funny.

One time the police came around and asked my dad who was buying bee-bees in the neighborhood. He had no idea about our little pranks. "All the kids buy them," he said.

But I was growing out of that kind of nonsense. I had found out about the accordion and that was taking up more and more of my time.

CHAPTER III

CHEESEBOX

School never meant anything to me. I suppose it was because my life was so full at home. I just wasn't interested in making any kind of emotional commitment to anything else. I didn't need anything else. About the only thing I got out of going to school is that I learned to speak English there.

The first school I went to was St. Mary's on Holmes Avenue. I went there for three grades and then transferred to William H. Brett public school when we moved to East 160th.

From there I went to Collinwood High School, which we called Five Points School in those days. I quit Collinwood when I was sixteen and went to Cleveland Trade School for a while.

Although I was an uninspired student, I always obeyed the teachers. You know how it was at that time. The teachers ranked somewhere between God and the hierarchy, and heaven help you if you were a bad boy in school.

Those teachers would wallop you with a paddle and if you complained to your parents they'd give it to you too. So I behaved. I can't remember ever getting into any kind of mischief. For one thing, I didn't want to be kept after school because my dad would have come down hard on me if I wasn't available to work at the hardware store.

My grades were just fair. I was good in arithmetic, but bad in English grammar. It was no wonder, considering the fact we never talked English at home.

I have always been proud of the fact, by the way, that I

speak good Slovenian today. To my way of thinking, anybody who's ashamed to talk the language of his ancestors is pretty much of a fool.

The only subjects I really liked in school were woodwork and cabinet making. They really intrigued me and came in handy later when I was a patternmaker.

Funny thing, but I was weak in music in school too, mostly because I wasn't interested. My music period came at the end of the day at Collinwood and whenever I had the chance I'd cut the class and go home early. I just didn't care for the modern kind of music we sang in school. I only wanted to listen to the old-time Slovene folk songs we sang at home.

Slovene music was more than just a sound. It represented a way of life. Everyone in the neighborhood grew up on it and stayed with it. It wasn't like today, when many ethnic youngsters gravitate to rock or country music.

You'd go to a wedding in those days and you'd see those gorgeous, spirited Slovenian girls gliding and whirling through the polka. The combination of these laughing girls and the music I loved made a lasting impression on me. I still think, by the way, that the Slovene polka, danced properly, is the prettiest dance on earth.

The neighborhood men, characterized by the boarders in our house, had the same kind of charisma for me. They were young, physical guys, brimming with vitality. They could drink, tell stories, joke with the girls and sing far into the night. Dressed immaculately in their white shirts, ties and hats, they carried a romantic, daring air.

It was no wonder that I wasn't interested in school. The prim schoolteachers looked pale and dry by comparison.

At the center of that lively Slovene community were the accordion players. We called them cheesebox players. They were, in a very real sense, the gods of the neighborhood. All activity revolved around them. Rudy Kozel and Frank Smith were a particularly well-known team in the area.

We had our own cheesebox hero in our house—Max Zelodec, one of the boarders. Max owned a button box made by Anton Mervar, a Slovenian immigrant who had a store at 6919 St. Clair. The store is still there today and is run by his daughter,

Justine. Beginning in 1915, the year I was born, Mervar handmade hundreds of beautiful button accordions. They had a contagious, tinny sound that no other button box could equal. Mervar would never tell what secret he had brought over from Europe that made his accordions so much better than anybody else's.

He took the secret to the grave with him when he and his wife were killed in a car crash in Salina, Kansas, in 1942. Mervar was only 57 at the time. When his son was told his parents had been killed, he died from shock. A triple funeral was held. Strangely enough, though Mervar was a genius at making those accordions, he never learned how to play one.

Anyway, Zelodec had a Mervar box. He paid a couple of hundred dollars for it. Today all the Mervar accordions are collectors' items and cost about $800 to buy, if you're lucky enough to find one for sale.

Zelodec, who worked as a mechanic, would invariably pick up his cheesebox after supper and the boarders would start singing. My father would always join in. I'd sit there quiet as a churchmouse and listen to them. They all had good voices. The more they drank, the better they sang.

I noticed Max controlled them with his accordion. If he played something fast, they sang fast. If he played something sweet and sentimental, they sang that way. He had power. He was the center of attention and the recipient of their compliments and the drinks they bought. I would watch every move he made on the keys.

I wasn't old enough to have my own cheesebox yet, but I'd pretend I was playing one on a little footstool we had in the kitchen. The stool was shaped about the size of an accordion and I'd pick it up and sing songs and make all the appropriate gestures, just as though I was playing.

Max would play for house weddings too and a lot of times I'd go with him to the job. I was proud to carry his accordion into the house for him and I always noticed that he'd be greeted with respect. He was a good-looking, stocky fellow, about 20 years old then.

Sometimes Max played so much that his left wrist would swell up from pulling the box. On hot nights, in that era when there was no air conditioning, he would keep a towel draped around his neck to catch the perspiration.

Between numbers, he drank leisurely and joked with the crowd. I decided I wanted to be like him.

I asked Max to teach me to play and he began giving me a few lessons. There were no notes for the button box. It was all by ear. I seemed to have a feel for it and caught on pretty quick. I practiced on Max's box during the day when he was at work. If some of the boarders were working nights and sleeping days, I'd have to practice in the garage. I was about nine years old then. I played strictly the songs Max played. Sometimes I couldn't find the right note and then I'd ask Max where it was when he came home and he would show me.

I improved so fast that I began to play a little for the boarders and neighbors. My dad, who loved the button box sound, was proud that I could play. I began to hope that pretty soon he would buy me my own accordion.

I got my wish through a tragedy—the suicide of a middle-aged neighborhood bachelor. The bachelor would come to our house and play balinca and have a few drinks. Sometimes, when he was short of money, my mom would give him credit.

One day the startling news came that he had turned the gas on in his apartment and killed himself. He lived alone above a garage on East 159th Street. His landlady, Mrs. Erzen, took care of his effects. She came to our house and asked my mother if he owed her any money.

He owed $75, so Mrs. Erzen suggested that my mother come to his apartment to see if there was anything she would like to have. My mother went there, saw the accordion, and brought it home for me.

That was when my playing really started to improve. I had that cheesebox with me all the time. When I went to work at the hardware store, I would take it with me on my little red wagon. If there were no customers I would practice in front of the store. People would walk by and encourage me, pat me on the head, and tell me I was a good little Slovenian.

When we played baseball on the street in front of our house, I'd keep the accordion on the porch. I'd play it when our side was batting and when it was my turn to bat I'd run down the steps to the plate. If I hit a home run I'd come back and bang out a particularly lively polka. If I made an out, I'd hurry back to the porch and play some more. The guys said it was nice to play ball with polka music in the background.

I began to get something of a reputation as an accordionist and people began inviting me to play at their lodge meetings. I was about fourteen then. I played for free. I was just happy to do it and to see that people liked my playing.

Having my own band never came to mind. I was crazy about the old-time songs and melodies, that's all. After I went to a wedding I could hear the accordion playing the songs in my head for two days.

I know now that I was a lucky young man to like anything that much. A lot of people go through life without having that kind of feeling for anything. If you don't mind my getting on the soapbox a little, I would say that's one of the major rules for success in life. Find something you like so well that you'll do it for nothing. Then, if you get paid for it, it's just an added bonus. It won't seem like work.

The first time I ever got paid for playing was at a lodge dance at Collinwood Slovenian Home on Holmes Avenue, where my father was a member of the board of directors. I think I got $5.

The dancers encouraged me as I played and they would say, "Frank, that's a little too fast," or "that's a little too slow." I listened to them and played the way they wanted it. Frank Skufca, one of my neighbors, accompanied me on the banjo.

By the time I was about fifteen, I felt I had really mastered the button box. I played three and four-fingered chords on every note, which isn't too easy to do. A lot of people will tell you even today that I am a great button box player, better at that than the piano accordion. Cleveland polka disc jockey Eddie Grosel insists I am the greatest button box player he's ever heard.

I still take the button box with me on jobs, but I only play it if people request it. I know there's a big button box revival going on now, but I feel it's only a novelty. That charming sound can get awfully tiresome if you hear it too much. Let's face it, the button box songs all sound pretty much alike.

The reason for that, as I explained before, is that the button box is limited. There are only certain songs you can play on it.

For that reason, I began to think of getting the more versatile piano accordion. I asked my father to buy me one, but he wouldn't hear of it. "All accordion players are bums," he said. He must have already feared that I was thinking of playing the accordion for a livelihood.

When I was sixteen, I saw an advertisement in the newspaper which said that a Mr. Joe Russ had a piano accordion for sale. He lived on Norwood, off St. Clair. I begged my mother to let me go and see the accordion. Finally she said, "All right, we'll go, but don't tell dad."

The next day my mother and I, accompanied by my sister Mary and her husband, Herman Kravos, went to see Mr. Russ. Herman drove us. Mr. Russ was one of those tall, sophisticated Slovenes. As I recall, he was a music teacher. The accordion was white, with a fancy design, the kind they don't make anymore. I thought it was beautiful.

Mr. Russ said he wanted $800 for it. My mother didn't argue. She just peeled $500 out of her purse and offered it to him. That was a lot of money in 1931. "Take it or leave it," she said. Mr. Russ saw that she meant business and took it. I had my piano accordion.

Mom didn't pay for the accordion entirely by herself, though. She informed my two other sisters, Rose and Josephine, who were still living at home, that they would have to chip in and help pay for it. She wanted a week's pay from each. Rose was working at Fisher Body for $50 a week, while Josephine earned $30 at Premier Vacuum Cleaner Co. on East 152nd Street.

Trouble was, after I got the accordion I couldn't take it home. My mother was afraid of what dad would say about spending so much money. She said I would have to keep the accordion at Mary's house, just a few doors away from us on East 160th. She said I'd have to practice there too. She also told me I better learn well because she had stuck out her neck for me.

So that was the way I began playing the piano accordion.

I was constantly at Mary's house (I had been an usher for her when she was married in 1930) and I was always practicing. When dad would come over to visit Mary, which was every day, I would hide the accordion and run out of the house. Dad would always say, "Where the hell is Frank always running?" This went on for months.

I was really having problems learning to play. Remember, I had to learn to read notes. It wasn't like the button box. Joe Notari gave me my first lessons, for about 50 cents apiece. He had a studio on Broadway and East 55th Street and I had to take two streetcars to get there. The first song Notari gave me to learn was "Good Night, Sweetheart." I couldn't get it. After one real bad lesson Notari told me I shouldn't bother to come back if I couldn't learn the song by the next lesson a week later.

That week was one of the toughest of my life. I felt I was at the crossroads. You know how kids overdramatize everything. I figured I had to learn that song or I was through. I'd have to give up and go back to the button box.

I practiced and practiced, but I couldn't get it. I was trying so hard I was crying. I'd come home late at night, eyes all red, and my mother would say, "Frankie, get some sleep. Look at you."

But I kept remembering that she had warned me to learn to play well. Otherwise my dad would never let me hear the end of it.

Finally, just when I was ready to give up, something clicked and everything fell into place. All at once I had it. I could play "Good Night, Sweetheart." Of all the thousands of songs I've played since then, I don't think I ever got a bigger thrill than I got when I played that song that night. I went home and slept the sleep of the untroubled.

After I graduated from Notari, I took some more lessons from Joe Trolli, a teacher in my neighborhood. I would say that altogether I had only about 25 lessons in my whole life.

I soon had enough confidence to face my father, who still didn't know that I had the piano box. I finally worked up enough courage to surprise him on a Christmas Eve. I figured he couldn't get too mad at me at that time of the year.

I waited until the drinks were flying and he was in a good mood. Then I just walked in and started playing one of his favorite Slovene waltzes. He listened, and then he walked up to me and put his hands on my shoulders and said, "I still like the cheesebox better. But if you're going to play it, play it well."

We had fun in those days, but it was the time of the Great Depression. The big thought in everybody's mind was to get work and make money. But jobs were real hard to come by. Things were so bad that dad eventually closed his hardware store. Nobody was buying anything.

When I was 19, a rumor went around that Fisher Body was hiring. So I went to Fisher Body every morning at 4 a.m. to get in the employment line first. The employment office opened at 9 a.m., but by then there would be hundreds of men standing in line. Then the employment manager would come out and say they weren't hiring that day. Everybody would put their hands in their pockets and walk slowly back to nowhere. The company could have put out a sign saying it wasn't hiring that day, but they never thought of that. Kids today just don't realize how tough things were in those days.

Finally, one day I got hired at Fisher Body. They wouldn't hire you unless you were 21, but I had already taken care of that little problem. My banjo player had given me his birth certificate. He was 21. When I was hired I used his name.

The superintendent took me to the foreman, who turned out to be my next door neighbor. He said, "Frank, what are you doing here? You're not 21." I leveled with him and told him what I'd done.

He was a good guy and didn't squeal on me. So they put me on the second shift, where I worked loading parts on the truck. My hands got all puffed up. On the third day, we went on strike and I was out of a job again.

This was the first time I ever heard of a strike. I didn't even know what it was all about. As I recall, they wanted to unionize the shop. They called them sit-down strikes in those days. When I got my paycheck for three days of work, incidentally, it was made out to my banjo player.

After that I looked for work again and landed a variety of low paying jobs. Most of them paid about 25 cents an hour. I worked at places like the A.B. Box Co., and at the Murray-Ohio Co., making bicycles.

I also made deliveries for Zalar's Collinwood Bakery and Spang's Bakery. That was probably my most enjoyable job in that period. My pay was $15, plus all I could eat. I drove the truck and made house-to-house deliveries of bread, cakes, pies and milk.

Sometimes, as I made my deliveries, I'd give a quick accordion lesson to some neighborhood boy who was learning to play. Nearly every house in Collinwood and on St. Clair had a small boy playing the cheesebox in those days.

On Friday nights, I played the accordion at Klaus' Tavern on West 131st Street. I'd finish playing there at 2:30 in the morning and had to make my first bakery deliveries at 4:30 in the morning. There wasn't time to go home, so I would just put on my bakery uniform at the tavern and go straight to work. The customers would leave their orders on notes in the milkbox.

CHAPTER IV

THE START

The 1930s were dynamite days for me, a blend of hard work and lots of fun. I didn't know it then, but I guess they were the best times of all. When you're working your way up, you always think you're struggling too hard and that the fight isn't worth it. Then, after you finally get somewhere, you realize that you were happiest when you were battling toward a goal. Believe me, it's a lot easier getting to the top than it is to stay there.

My first bands were composed of fellows such as Skufca on banjo, Lee Novak on drums, Al Naglitch on piano, Jim Hocevar, guitar, and Bill Dunlavey on saxophone. I was never too crazy about using a horn in the band though. In later years I never used a sax. I just didn't believe they belonged with the kind of music I play. I had nothing against Dunlavey though. In fact, he was one of my ushers when I got married the first time.

Me and the Yanks built our reputation gradually. We played weddings for $1 an hour, or $5 for four hours. We were glad to get it.

We played a lot in the old St. Clair neighborhood, around East 65th Street. Our two big spots there were Grdina's Twilight Ballroom and the Slovenian National Home. When you played the National Home you felt you were in the big time.

The National Home had then, and still has today, a big, beautiful ballroom. Two elegant pillars decorated by mirrors give it a distinctive look. Lodge dances were held there every Friday, Saturday and Sunday, and sometimes as many as a thousand people would attend from all over the city.

They would come in by streetcar, and every 15 minutes a crowd of 50 or so would surge at once through the dance hall door. We could see them come in from the stage and we'd say, "Oh, oh, another streetcar just came in."

Very few people had dates at those dances. They were gathering places. The girls would come with their girlfriends and the men would come with their buddies. The girls would sit down together, then dance together. They would pretend not to notice the young men, who would stand in a giant stag line all around the floor.

The guys would usually go to the bar to fuel up their courage. When they had enough, they'd come out and compete for the girls. A girl who danced with everyone who asked her was very popular and always had a lot of dances. The shy guys knew they could approach her without fear of being turned down.

The girls who were snooty and only danced with the good-looking guys had more trouble. If they turned down too many guys, all but the most confident stags would notice and stay away from them for fear of being embarrassed. It was tough to ask a girl for a dance, be rejected, and then go back to your buddies and say, "She said she didn't want to dance this one."

Naturally, this combination of music, booze and young blood made for a lot of fights. As accordionist Lou Trebar once said, we used to watch the corners from our vantage point on the stage. Sometimes there would be a fight going on in each one.

But by and large, the National Home is a place fondly remembered by many, many people. Countless men and women from all over Cleveland met their future wives and husbands there, while countless others had their hearts broken.

And how those kids could dance. Weaned on the polka, they executed steps that are beyond the ability of most polka dancers today. You'd see them do the full pivot (in my opinion the most graceful, difficult step in ballroom dancing) the half pivot and the reverse turn. I haven't seen anybody do a full pivot around a big hall in years.

When you'd see it done perfectly by a Slovene pair that looked like Cary Grant and Lana Turner it could take your breath away. And you'd play just a little better on the stage.

After the dances, the frolics would continue at places like the old Metropole Cafe on East 55th, or at the Top Hat Tavern, across the street from the National Home. Eddie Simms, the famed boxer, owned the Top Hat, acting as his own comedian, accordionist and bouncer.

Sometimes, on winter nights after the bars closed, we'd ride bobsleds up and down St. Clair.

The first bar I played at was the Gay Inn, on St. Clair and East 70th. It was owned by an old family friend, John Simcic, the balinca star. When John hired me to play for him I was working as a patternmaker at Westeel Castings on East 70th. I'd stop in his place for lunch and one day he asked me if I wanted to play there on a Friday night.

I accepted. The pay was $15 for three pieces. Novak and Skufca came with me. The first Friday we didn't do too well, but the next two weeks the joint was jammed. The same thing happened when I played at the Gaiety Bar on Waterloo.

That was what made me start thinking. I was playing and working hard and the guys who owned the bars were making all the money. I was playing for $5 and spending maybe $10 at the bar. I began to think of opening my own bar and playing in it. But that was still in the future. There was too much fun to be had first.

We had a cheerful bunch in the band—I never could stand to have any sourpusses playing with me—and people would follow us around wherever we went. I had a lot of friends because I always made it a point to mingle with the people at intermissions, and I always tried to consider the older people.

There were some bands who didn't give a darn about the old timers. They'd play a lot of jitterbug numbers and the Big Apple, a popular American dance then. But I always kept an eye out for the elders and played the polkas and waltzes nice and easy. As it turned out, that gave me a style all my own.

In all honesty, we were probably the most popular polka band in town. Shorty Callister had a good outfit and so did Louie Spehek, and Pecon and Trebar had already begun. The legendary Matt Hoyer was still around, but past his peak.

But we consistently outdrew those groups. I think one reason was that we had more personality. We got that idea from Jackie Zorc, one of the old cheesebox masters.

Zorc was one of the best players ever, and on top of that he had a great smile. He always smiled when he played, which was a departure from the old style guys, who would sit down and play, always with dignified looks on their faces. I thought Zorc was the most fun, and I imitated him, smiling widely. Then I added another touch, and stood up and bounced around the stage. I think I was the first polka bandleader to play that way.

I'd always tell the guys, "C'mon, let's act like we're alive, like we're having a good time." It made a big difference. I have to thank Zorc for that. By the way, after Zorc got married he pretty much quit playing. He didn't want to make a career out of it. A lot of people think he was the best accordion player Cleveland has ever had.

It was about this time that we started the Wrong Club, made up of a bunch of young guys who liked polkas. We took the name because we didn't want to be taken seriously. We only wanted to have fun.

We held dances on Saturday nights at Glenridge Barn in what is now Indian Hills in Euclid, Ohio, outside Cleveland. We were an aggressive club, selling tickets to people in bars and dance halls all week long. Come Saturday we'd have as many as 1,200 people.

Not too many young guys had cars at that time, so people would come to our dances or to picnics at Pintar's Farm in trucks rented from the Oblak Moving Company. Old Mr. Oblak would stack maybe 100 young guys and girls in his truck and charge them 25 cents apiece for the ride back and forth from St. Clair. He'd stay at the picnic or dance himself and have a good time too, then drive everybody home. Sometimes you'd have more fun going home on Oblak's truck than you had at the picnic, with all the singing and laughing.

Me and the Yanks would play up in the loft of the barn during the Wrong Club dances. We used money from the profits to buy ourselves band uniforms. We had two uniforms, one a blue suit with exceptionally fine material, and the other a powder blue jacket with black satin lapels. We even bought black shoes and socks to match.

We also used the money from the Wrong Club profits to go on outings, swimming, roller skating and horseback riding.

I don't know, I wasn't afraid of anything in those days. Anything for a laugh. We went swimming once at Nelson's Ledges and we all got drunk. I jumped into the lake off a canoe. Trouble was, I had never bothered to learn how to swim. I was having a great time, but the guys got scared when I began going under. Al Jalen, who was later to become my best man, jumped in and fished me out.

I was a practical joker too and Lee Novak, my drummer, was one of my favorite targets. Lee was about four years older than me, wore glasses and was a sensible, serious guy. I guess that was why I liked to have fun with him.

At one of the Wrong Club dances, I wired his new car. When he started it, it exploded, making a lot of noise and smoke and whistling. Lee ran like hell when it went off. The cops came running and everybody had a big laugh.

Another time we went horseback riding in Willoughby. I went up to the owner of the horses, pointed at Lee and said, "See that tall guy over there? He can really ride. Give him your wildest horse." Lee, of course, had never been on a horse in his life.

Well, the owner brought out this big, black horse and he was snorting and stomping, raring to go. Lee was a little worried, but started to get up on him from the right side. The owner yelled, "Hey, you're getting up on the wrong side." We were all laughing so hard we had to hold our sides.

Lee finally got up on the horse, who by this time knew he had a patsy. The horse stood up on his hind legs and took off on a gallop, with Lee yelling and holding on for dear life. The owner went out after him and brought Lee in. Then he gave him a nice, slow horse and we all went trotting out, real easy.

But after a while, I had to get off my horse and go behind a tree to answer Mother Nature. While I was in the woods, Lee kicked my horse in the rear and the horse took off and ran right back to the stable. I had to walk all the way back. Lee got even with me that time.

Later that same day, we saw a beautiful girl with another lively horse. Somebody said she was a racketeer's mistress. She looked hard-nosed, all right, but she looked sharp too. I tried to make an impression on her, show off a little. That was my style. I asked her if I could pose for a picture with her and the horse. She said okay, and I suggested she make the horse rear up. When he did, I jumped under the horse's legs and Novak took the picture. The girl might have been impressed, but it didn't make any difference. I never saw her again.

Novak saved my can once. It was in Niles, Ohio, where we were playing for a dance. It was a pretty wild night. There was a big fight in the middle of it, with one guy biting off another guy's thumb. That's the kind of crowd it was.

After the job we were getting off the bandstand and some cocky Italian made a remark about the hat I was wearing. It was one of those Joe College, pork-pie hats. I answered him back with some wise guy words and pretty soon we were swinging at each other. I ripped the guy's shirt.

Novak got in between us and shoved me into the car. Then he grabbed the Italian and tried to cool him down. The Italian said to him, "You're lucky you're wearing glasses. I can't hit you. It's a penitentiary offense to hit a guy who wears glasses.

People really believed things like that in those days. They may have been tough, but they had a certain sense of fair play. Today it's no holds barred in a fight. They'd hit your grandmother with brass knuckles if they had to.

We were softball players too. We played the fast pitch variety of the game, not the slow pitch stuff that's so popular today. We thought slow pitch was for girls and little boys.

I was the team manager and I used to be tough on the players. I didn't want any nonsense. We were playing at Gordon Park one time and some neighborhood girls came to watch. Patsy Krall, who grew up with me and went everywhere with me, was talking to them during the pre-game warmup. He had driven to the game with me in my 1937 Chevrolet.

I told Patsy twice to stop talking to the girls and go shag flies in the outfield. He said he would but kept talking. So I got mad and scratched him from the starting lineup. Boy, was he mad. After the game he was still fuming and he started to walk home. But I came after him in the car and said, "C'mon in. You deserved it." He came in and we went home.

Patsy was the key man in a game we still talk about today when we get together. We were playing for the Loyalites in the championship game of the old Inter-Lodge League, composed of various Slovene fraternal groups. The game was at Glenview Field, north of the Lake Shore Boulevard on East 100th Street. That's in a black neighborhood now. It was the first night game they ever had there and a big crowd was on hand. We felt like big shots going in to play night softball.

I was just a fair player, but I had a couple of hits that game and so did Patsy. We had a 5-2 lead in the sixth inning of the seven-inning game. Patsy told me he had to leave then because he had to go bowling in some league. It was the opening night of the league. I told him he could go. What the heck, we had a good lead and the game was almost over.

I put in Frank Zupan to replace Krall in right field and a popper fell in between him and me. I played second base. Then another one dropped in and there were a couple more hits. Then Al Jalen hit one over Zupan's head to win the game. Krall would have had the ball because he knew how to play Jalen.

The next day I saw Patsy and he said, "Well, it feels nice to be the champs." He thought we'd won. I said, "Don't even talk to me." It took me a couple of days to get over it. I was furious. I'll never let Patsy forget that one.

Thinking back on all that's happened since then, I know how silly I was to get mad about a ball game. But that's how young guys are. It's when you don't get mad anymore about losing a ball game or missing a four-foot putt that you know you're getting old.

I was always very active in the Slovene lodges and I'm still a member today. I took my cue from my dad, who sold advertisements door-to-door for years for the Prosveta, the Slovene National Benefit Society's newspaper. I was president of the Loyalites and the American Mutual Life Association's Betsy

Ross Lodge. I was also in the American Fraternal Union's Eastern Stars, another Slovene lodge.

Music was never far away. The Loyalites formed a singing group and the guys would come to my house and sing in the basement. I remember guys like Joe Anzlovar, Frank Ciligoj and Tony Kastelic coming over. I also joined the Soca Singing Society, which performed concerts and operettas. I went to the Soca rehearsals every Thursday for two or three years.

I got my first big break musically around 1932, when Dr. James Malle, a dentist, invited me to play on his Sunday radio program on WJAY. Malle had the first Slovenian radio show in Cleveland. When he left the show Charles Zorman and then Martin Antoncic (Heinie Martin) took over.

We played every Sunday on the radio for years. All the music was live then. Taped shows were unheard of. We weren't paid much, but those jobs put us on the map. There were only four radio stations in Cleveland then, with no FM radio and no television. Everybody listened to the radio. We got terrific exposure.

When Heinie switched to WGAR radio we went with him, but we ran into some union trouble. At that time, the station had an eight-piece live band, featuring a violin, that played for all the nationality programs, German, Polish, Czech, Slovak, what-have-you. Their music was excellent, but they didn't know enough Slovene music, which was what Heinie wanted to play on his show. Heinie wanted my band to play, but the Musicians Union said we couldn't because we weren't in the union. I hadn't joined because I still wasn't sure if I wanted to make a career out of music.

Heinie insisted he wanted me on the show and he arranged a compromise with the union. He pointed out that the eight-piece band didn't know enough Slovene music and that he needed me. The union agreed to let me write arrangements for the eight-piece band, and play the accordion too. My other band members weren't allowed to play, though. That was when Joe Trolli and I first began writing music.

Heinie's Slovenian radio show became an institution and lasted for 35 years before he retired to Florida a few years back. When the Slovenian man of the year functions were started, he was the first man to be honored. He is a great guy, never knocks anybody, and is always willing to help you. I first met him when he was the manager of the St. Clair Recreation Center, or Bathhouse. I played for him for free at his community variety shows long before I went on the radio with him.

I got into car trouble with the police for the second time in my life during my radio period. It happened in 1935, on my parents' 25th wedding anniversary.

We were having a celebration at home when I suddenly realized I was going to be late for the 6 o'clock radio show. I jumped into my car and sped downtown. I crashed four lights before the police pinched me.

The next day I had to go to court and the judge gave me a unique sentence. He let me go without a fine on the condition that I play six times for free at various orphanages. I was glad to do it.

Heinie Martin also got me started in the recording business. People kept asking me to make a record and Heinie thought it would be a good idea. We were getting to be pretty well-known.

So, in 1938, Heinie took me and the Yanks to the Cleveland Recording Company studios downtown, on Huron Road. The studio was owned by Fred Wolf, who had a Bohemian radio show on WGAR. I put up all the money for the recording session out of my own pocket.

We cut two 78 rpm records on the Yankee label. The songs were "The Silk Umbrella Polka," "Always Jolly," which was my dad's favorite, a Slovene waltz medley and an old song called "Hooray Slovenes." We still weren't members of the musicians union, so to avoid trouble we left our names off the record. On the disc it merely said the music was by the Slovene Folk Orchestra. That was me, Novak, Skufca and Naglitch.

We took the records to Mervar's store on St. Clair, the same Mervar who made those great accordions. He had a big record store and it was the only one in town that sold Slovene records. Fast as he got ours, he sold them. All 4,000 went in a couple of weeks.

The next year we recorded four more sides, with me paying

all expenses again. This time the songs were on the Joliet label, and we called our band the Jolly Yugoslavs. They sold out fast again.

People liked our sound, but aside from that I think one reason the records sold so well was that no Slovene records had been made in the United States since Josephine Lausche and Mary Udovic recorded their classic song duets in the late 1920s.

The Depression killed the Slovene record business after that for about ten years. We came along when the time was right, with people panting for some good new Slovene records. Give Heinie Martin credit for knowing the public was ready.

A word here about the famed Lausche-Udovic team. They recorded in New York with the full 32-piece Columbia recording orchestra backing them up. This is something that just isn't done in the polka field anymore.

On top of that they were outstanding singers, with Mary Udovic an incomparable soprano and Josephine Lausche blending perfectly with her alto. They were young Cleveland women who sang at all the Slovene affairs. I doubt if they ever were paid anything. They sang for the pure joy of it. Their matchless recordings are collectors' items today. Numerous duets have come along and tried to emulate them, but there was only one Lausche-Udovic combination. Their sentimental songs could tear your heart out.

Miss Udovic died in 1965, but Josephine Lausche Welf, now over 80, is still alive and well. She lives quietly in Euclid, a suburb of Cleveland. I think it would be just great if Josephine would be honored with a testimonial of some kind by the Slovene people. I even think it would be nice if she was installed in the Polka Hall of Fame, along with her great partner.

Mrs. Welf, by the way, is a sister of former Senator Lausche. Another brother was William (Doc) Lausche, a dentist who wrote the music to some of the most lasting polka classics. What a remarkable family.

Many people consider Doc to be the originator of the American-style polka music. His melodies have been recorded scores of times and are still being copied today. Doc made the arrangements and played a superb piano on the Lausche-

Udovic records. He died in 1967. In my opinion, he also belongs in the Hall of Fame.

Doc was my dentist, incidentally. He always had his mind on music, though. He would be drilling your tooth and whistling a tune you'd never heard before. You'd ask him what it was and he'd say, "It's a new song I'm working on."

One more record I made in those early days deserves mention. It featured my two little nieces, Dorothy and Rose Kravos, who sang a couple of old Slovene folk tunes. The girls were only about nine and eleven years old then.

It was my idea to put the girls on the record. We had never had a vocal on a disc before and I thought it might be a good idea. I had heard the girls sing at my sister Mary's house. Mary would teach them one line of a Slovene folk song every day and I would come over every night after supper and play for them as they sang. If they went off key, I'd make them start all over.

Anyway, the girls had a cute sound and I thought it was worth the chance to have them record. I figured that nobody would criticize them anyway if they flopped because they were kids. But they didn't flop. They were terrific.

People have knocked my accordion playing occasionally, but they all admit I can pick talent.

CHAPTER V

JUNE

There was an old saying in our neighborhood: A boy gets his brains from his father but he gets his heart from his mother. The women were the most important people in our community. They ran the households, dictated the way we lived and had the most respect.

But it was the men who had the fun. We caroused together, drank together and depended on each other for most of our good times. But we wanted to be ladies' men too.

There was one sure way to qualify. All you had to do was be a sharp dresser and a good dancer. Many a mother would say to a bashful son: "What's wrong with you? Why don't you learn to dance? Nobody will want to marry you." As a result, even the clumsiest youths in the neighborhood learned to dance a pretty good waltz and polka.

When I think back to our social lives in those days, it seems to me that the one big difference between then and now was in our dating habits. When I was young, we didn't go out with girls unless it was for keeps. Most of the time we went out in groups, to dances, picnics, and weddings. If a couple clicked, they would then pair off and begin going together solo.

It wasn't like today, when a date can be as casual as a handshake. When you took a girl out in 1935, it probably meant that you were thinking of marrying her.

I'm not saying the old custom was better. It probably wasn't. We made too big a thing out of dating and it could put a lot more pressure on you. Bashful fellows were often reluctant to take out girls alone because they knew it would start the whole neighborhood gossiping about a possible romance.

A lot of guys couldn't stand the thought of being shot down by a girl after a few dates. They knew the news would be all over the street. So they saved themselves a lot of grief and just stayed with the boys and had their card games and balinca matches and singing.

That, plus the fact the Slovene mothers made it so convenient for their sons to live at home, may explain why so many Slovenes on Collinwood and St. Clair remained bachelors.

I had my share of fun with girls, I guess. The first one that meant anything to me lived near St. Clair. She was a cute, short Slovene girl.

She was about 17 and I was a couple of years older. For a while, I wanted to marry her, but my folks, especially my mother, objected. There was some kind of family misunderstanding. In those days you didn't just marry each other. You married each other's family too.

I had another romance with a Cleveland girl. I was crazy about her for a time. She was very attractive and about five feet, six inches tall, which was pretty tall for those days.

I asked her to marry me, but she refused. After that I totally lost interest in her. I was never one to carry a torch. My feeling was that there were plenty of fish in the ocean.

For a long time I went with a girl who lived in Collinwood. She was a double for Alice Faye, the movie star. I met her when I was playing for a wedding and she was one of the bridesmaids.

I got to know her better through my bakery route. I delivered to her house and her mother would invite me in for a cup of coffee. We would chat in Slovenian. Her mother really liked me and wanted her to marry me. My whole family wanted me to marry her too.

I took her to all the best places and treated her like a queen. In fact, if you talk to any of my old girl friends they'll tell you that I was always a gentleman. I took her to a fancy night club, The Southern Tavern, on Carnegie and East 105th Street, and for cruises on Lake Erie. Another time we spent a whole day at Geauga Lake. Once I took her with me when I played a job at the Twilight Gardens, and I came off the bandstand and danced a few dances with her.

Yankovic bridal party, 1940 (left to right): Emily and Tony Yankovic (Frank's cousins), Ann Skala, Al Jalen (best man), June and Frank, Josephine Yankovic (Frank's sister), and Bill Dunlavey.

The Yankovic Family in 1954. Clockwise, from right: Linda (at the piano), Mark, Jerry, Andrea, June with Johnny on her lap, Frank, Jr., Frank, and Richard. Robbie was born the next year.

LOYALITES 2ND ANNUAL FIELD DAY - JULY 4th 1941 - S.N.P.J. FARM.

Martin Antoncic, the Cleveland radio broadcaster who started Yankovic on his radio and recording career.

Frank in Glasgow in 1945 when entertaining troops.

We talked about getting married, but she decided against it because I was a musician. She felt that it would be too tough a life, that she would always be waiting around for me.

So she married a fine man and, they had two girls. But after they had been married about twelve years, he was killed by a hit-skip driver. When I heard about it I telephoned her and offered her any help I could. Later on she remarried. I understand she's very content.

But don't get the idea from all this that I was a wolf. I had too much pride in myself to chase women. I liked them but I wouldn't make a fool of myself. I was a friendly guy and mingled with all the people at the dances we played. Some of them, naturally, were pretty girls.

I finally met the girl I was looking for in 1939, while playing for Joe Anzlovar's wedding on East 160th Street. It was at Pauline Mauser's house. Tony Fortuna introduced us. Her name was June Erwerthe and she was of French, Irish and Austrian descent.

I thought June was a real doll and I flipped. I never felt anything go through my system like it did on that night.

June was 17, about five feet, three inches tall, with a perfect skin. She was a great dancer and had a quick, agile way of carrying herself.

She had a free, open personality and sometimes she gave me the impression she didn't care what she looked like, as though beauty wasn't important. She would be careless about her appearance, forgetting to comb her hair, for instance. I had the feeling she was a wild filly. But when she chose she could be as charming and polished as if she'd gone to finishing school.

When you put everything together, she was a knockout. Her photographs have never really done her justice. A camera can't capture personality.

I asked her if I could take her home after the wedding that night, but she turned me down. She said I would have to come to her house if I wanted to take her out on a date. She had come to the wedding with some girlfriends. I found out later that she was going more or less steady at the time with another Slovenian.

I went home alone that night but I felt I had made a great discovery. I felt like I was in heaven just talking to her.

I was living at home yet and my roommate was Tony Drenik, the boarder who later married my sister Rose. We slept in the same bed. I got home at three in the morning and I was so high on romance I had to talk with somebody.

I shook poor Tony awake and said, "I met an angel tonight. I can't forget her. That's the girl I'm going to marry."

Tony didn't appreciate the news. He said, "That's good. Now go to sleep."

One of our first dates was at the National Home. I was playing a job there, so I sent Al Jalen to pick her up in my Chevrolet. She lived on Whittier Avenue in the Hough neighborhood. It was a nice neighborhood then, but it's pretty run down now. You might remember the Hough race riots of 1966, where four people were killed. Go through Hough today and it looks like they just had a war.

June sat in front of the stage that night while I played. I directed all my attention toward her. During the intermissions we talked. Jalen and Krall danced with her all night as a favor to me. I didn't want everybody and his uncle chasing after her.

Afterward we went to Hatton's Restaurant on East 55th Street for hamburgers and malted milks. It wasn't like today, where kids go to supper clubs for $25 meals. I don't know, everything changed about twenty years ago. It seemed like everybody got rich and fancy.

June still went out with her old boyfriend a few times, but then broke up with him completely. We got hooked on each other and everything happened very fast. My parents weren't too happy, however. They wanted me to marry a Slovene girl.

But June did impress my dad once when she came to our house. My dad was sitting on the porch and his eyes popped when he saw her step out of a taxicab. In dad's way of thinking, only rich people could afford a cab.

Later on he told everybody, "Boy, my son Frankie's going to marry a rich woman. She rides taxis."

That was one of June's traits. She always wanted to go first class and money meant nothing to her. I found that out as the years went by.

I also found out that she could be a spitfire. She never trusted me. I remember one night when me and the Yanks were practicing at Lee Novak's house at 1200 Norwood Road. Skufca, Novak and I would play our songs there and people could hear us out on the street. People loved to sit on porches and listen. There wasn't much else to do in those pre-television days.

We finished practicing and I had to go pick June up. I was a little late and I hurried out. But I just missed her. She arrived at Novak's house in a cab five minutes later. She charged through the front gate and past the porch, where a lot of people were sitting and talking. Then she burst into Novak's house in the backyard and yelled, "Where's Frankie?"

When he told her I had just left she zoomed right out again. She was always worried that I was going to visit my first girlfriend. Whenever I was late I always blamed Novak and told her I was out with him. Or I'd tell her I was with Krall, Jalen or Ulrich Lube. They traveled around with us and went to all our dances.

Another incident took place when SNPJ Farm opened in 1940. We played the very first dance they held there. It's a popular picnic and dance area for Cleveland Slovenes, and it's still thriving.

Some of the guys decided to play a joke on me and brought a beautiful redhead to the dance. I was at the bar with June having a beer and the redhead walked up to me, took the beer out of my mouth and drank it. She just smiled and never said a word to me, as though we were old friends. Then she hugged me and kissed me on the mouth.

When June saw this she slapped me in the face and started screaming at me. It was the week before our wedding. I had a hard time convincing her I'd never seen the girl before.

But I was jealous too. I suppose we had what you would call a stormy romance.

June had studied the violin for years and knew how to sing. So when she asked me if she could sing a bit with us I said okay. She was a pretty good canary, and she'd sing a few numbers with us every night. Her big hit was "You Must Have

Been a Beautiful Baby." She did great on it. She even sang a little Slovenian—phonetically.

After she'd sing, she would go on the dance floor. I'd get mad if she looked like she was having too much fun with one guy. It seemed like her old boyfriend was around too much. If it looked like she was getting too frisky, I'd call her back on the stage to sing. I was mad, so I'd yell at her. "Get closer to the microphone, damn it," I'd shout. She'd argue back. With the mike right there, you could hear us all over the floor.

She wasn't afraid of me, that was for sure. Once we were playing in Milwaukee and June was with us. It was a great weekend trip, with a lot of people coming along just for the fun of it. It was before we were married, so June slept in the hotel room with my sister Josephine. I slept with some of the guys.

On Sunday morning June woke up and saw she had a snag in her stockings. She came to my room and asked me to go out and buy her a new pair. I told her she didn't need them and she grabbed an ashtray and threw it at my head. It just missed me. It was that kind of spirit that I found irresistible. It should have been the tipoff for what was to follow.

June and I were married in St. Mary's Church in Collinwood on July 13, 1940. I was 25 and she was 18, although I didn't find that out until much later. She told me she was 20.

Al Jalen was my best man and the ushers were Dunlavey and my cousin, Tony Yankovic. We visited about 15 to 20 houses of relatives and friends during the afternoon, in the old Slovene custom.

Joe Lasicky made the rounds with us, playing the accordion, and wherever we stopped people would give us something to eat and drink. By the time the reception began at my parents' house that evening the wedding party was feeling very good.

It was a small reception and everybody had a jolly time. Max Zelodec played and we had a pillow dance. We didn't want to hurt people's feelings by not inviting them, so we deliberately kept it a small wedding. We only invited relatives and very close friends.

After the wedding June and I went on a one-week honeymoon to Niagara Falls and Virginia. Then we settled down in our first house, at 1272 East 172nd Street. I was working as a patternmaker, teaching the accordion at $1 an hour, and working my usual dances, weddings and night clubs. June always came along and sat in front of the stage. We were very happy.

In 1941 I decided to go into the tavern business. I had been watching the saloon operators rake in the money while I played long enough. I really got the idea when I played at the Gaiety Bar in Collinwood. A fellow named Polc owned the place and he couldn't even speak English. Not a word. I was loading the joint for him every weekend and I figured maybe I could do the same for myself. Besides, I was about to become a father. It takes money to raise kids.

We bought the tavern at 528 East 152nd Street from a Croatian named Juratovic. My sister Josephine, and her husband, Tom Milakovich, were my partners. Dad loaned us $6,000 to buy the place and eventually we paid back every cent. I still remember when he gave us the money. He went to this big safe he kept in his kitchen. It was about three feet high. When he opened it, we saw it was stuffed with money. Like a lot of old Slovenes, dad didn't trust banks.

We opened the tavern in November 1941, about a week before my first child, Linda, was born. I had no experience in the bar business, but I was willing to work. And work I did. I was the chief bartender, chef and cleaning man, and I also played the accordion.

My musician friends all thought I was making a big mistake going into the bar business. I broke the news to them one afternoon at the Metropole Bar on East 55th, where all the musicians always got together for Sunday jam sessions. Everybody thought I was crazy. They couldn't understand why I wanted to go into the bar business when I had the most popular band in town. They predicted I'd get so wrapped up in being a saloon keeper that I'd soon lose interest in music. They also pointed out that I'd have too much competition. The Metropole was the hottest polka spot in town, but there were a couple of other big ones too—the First and Last Chance Bar on East 165th and St. Clair and the Rendezvous Bar on

West 25th. Pete Sokach, a good accordion man, was the mainstay at the First and Last Chance.

There was so much controversy about my going into business that I called a meeting of my band members – Novak, Dunlavey and Naglitch. I told them they could stay with me if they wanted, but that they should feel free to quit if they didn't want to play in my place all the time. Novak and Dunlavey left me. Naglitch stayed.

For three or four weeks it looked like I'd made a big mistake. Business was awful. Then all of a sudden everybody started coming in. The place turned over and became the hangout for musicians like Pecon, Eddie Habat, Johnny Vadnal, Hokey Hokavar, Kenny Bass and all the others.

Musicians attract girls. Girls attract good spenders. The joint was really jumping.

Nobody enjoyed himself more there than Habat. He was a regular in that bar from the time he was 14. He was a brash, friendly kid and he loved to play the accordion. His older brother, Johnny, who is now a schoolteacher, thought the world of him. He loved the way he played. But Johnny wanted Eddie to pay more attention to school and he hoped he'd go to college.

One night the two of them were both in the saloon. People were standing four deep at the bar, singing and laughing. Eddie was the center of attention, banging out the polkas. At the height of the evening, Eddie turned to his brother and said, "Look at this. Why should I go to college? I don't need anything. Everything I want in the whole world is right here."

Once, we got into trouble with the State men. Somebody sold booze to a minor and we were closed down. I got in touch with a lawyer and asked for advice. He told me he could get the case taken care of through a big Cleveland politician. The lawyer said, though, that in return I would have to buy 75% of all the beer we used from then on from a brewery the politician owned. I agreed and the case was settled. As I recall we got off with a lesser fine.

We ran a real nice family business. My mom and sisters would clean up and make lunches and June worked as a waitress. Herman Kravos, Tom Milakovich and Frank Spilar would help out at the bar.

Dad would open the bar every morning, go to the bank and cash checks. He was there so much that people thought the place was his. They still do, in fact. Every once in a while I run into somebody who tells me he first heard me playing at my dad's bar. Dad was also great company for the drinkers. He loved to tell jokes and sing. He had a very happy old age.

(Eventually, I bought out Tom and Josephine and became sole owner. Josephine, by the way, is the only one of my sisters who's not living. She died in 1965, the day before her daughter Marilyn's wedding. She went out to buy a pair of shoes with my mother and Dorothy Kravos and collapsed and died of a heart attack in the car. The wedding was postponed and was held two weeks later without a reception.)

We held our grand opening at the club on December 6, 1941, the day before the Japanese bombed Pearl Harbor and threw the United States into war.

It wasn't long before I went into the army and encountered a disaster that almost cost me my life.

CHAPTER VI

WAR

When the war started the army gave me a low number in the draft. Uncle Sam was taking almost every able-bodied man from age 17 to 45, so I figured I'd be going in soon. I was only 26. But time went on and I didn't get a call.

In those days there was a lot of patriotic feeling. People talked about each man doing his part for the war effort. If you weren't in the service, you were expected to at least be working in a defense plant. I started to hear some criticism, so even though I was plenty busy in our bar, I went to Fisher Body and got a job in the machine shop. I operated a giant punch press that stamped out complete car tops. That press was about five stories high. It was the first one they used on cars. Before that, all car tops were made of wood.

I worked the third shift at Fisher Body. I would work in the bar until 11 o'clock at night, then go to the shop and work there until 7 in the morning. It was a man-killing schedule.

But Fisher Body had hired so many extra people to handle all the defense work that the foremen didn't know which end was up. Guys were stumbling all over each other, getting paid good money for standing around and doing nothing.

I was doing hardly any work. In fact, I didn't even know who my foreman was. So, after a few days, I figured there was no sense in just standing around. I could just as well stay at home if I wasn't going to work.

So I came up with a system. I'd leave the bar, punch in at Fisher Body, and go home. Then, at seven in the morning, I'd go back to Fisher Body and punch out.

This went on for two or three months. When they found me out, they fired me, naturally.

After that I went to work at Thompson Products as an external grinder. There were no shenanigans there. I worked every night. My boss was Frank Novak, the button box player, who years later made a very successful record with me. Novak was in charge of the whole machine shop.

All during this time, business was really booming in the bar. The war had finally ended the Depression and people were flocking in with money in their pockets. All the factories were going full blast and everybody was working six days a week. Our little bar, which could handle 150 people, was getting too small for all the action. So we decided to go to a bigger place.

We bought a commercial building across the street, which had four stores in it. It had to be completely rebuilt into a night club. I gave the contract to Demshar Builders, and they went to work, tearing down the walls.

But, because of the war, steel was hard to come by. It was like pulling teeth. With the job half done, Demshar said he couldn't finish. He couldn't get the steel to put up the beams. So there I was—stuck with a half-finished building. What to do?

Somebody put me in touch with a Jewish builder. He told me not to worry. He said he'd take care of things. I had to give him an extra $40,000, but sure enough, he got the building put up. I don't know what kind of strings he pulled. They put the steel beams up at night, so nobody could see them working. During the day they were covered up by big canvasses.

The new building was great for business, but sometimes I think maybe I never should have gone across the street. We were happy in our first little bar and maybe things would have worked out all different if we just stayed there. We were making a good buck and had no headaches. When we went into the bigger place, our business increased, but so did our overhead. We had more pressure all around.

In the meantime, I was active again with my band. I still had the travel bug. I couldn't stay tied down. We'd play in the club and we'd also make weekend trips around Ohio, Michigan and Pennsylvania. It was then that I started hearing rumors about June.

I'd talk to June about it and she would deny everything. But I could tell there was something going on. I could see there was a change in our marriage after about the first six months.

I wrestled with the situation in my mind. Looking back, I don't think June ever really loved me. I think she was only in love with the idea of being married to me because I was a musician. I was living a kind of life that seemed glamorous to her. Don't forget, she was only 18 years old. I don't think she was ready to settle down yet.

I've often regretted that I didn't get a divorce right then or when I came home from the army. But I was from an old-fashioned family and you have to remember the way things were then. Divorce was considered a big scandal. In those days people would stay married to each other for fifty years even if they hated each other. Now it's different. A lot of nice people get divorced and nobody thinks anything of it. I think the new way makes sense.

Nevertheless, all the time my mother was alive I didn't want to even think of getting a divorce. I knew it would break her heart. Nobody in the family had ever been divorced and I didn't want to be first.

The war went on for over a year and still I didn't hear from the draft board, probably because I was married and had two kids. Frankie Jr. had arrived by then.

People were talking a lot and it bothered me. They were saying, "What's the matter? Are you a goldbricker?" Things like that. They pretended they said it as a joke, but deep down I knew they meant it.

I was always one who cared what people thought about me. I wanted respect. So one day I went to the draft board and told them I didn't want to be exempt from the draft just because I had a family. I said I wanted to be called in.

I was supposed to be inducted February 17, 1943, but the army gave me an extra month to take care of my night club affairs. On March 17, 1943, I went into the army. On the night before, I had one of the most emotional experiences of my life. It centered around June.

Don't get the idea that June and I were totally unhappy

before I went into the service. As I said, we had problems, but there were a lot of good times too. I was in love with her and I was hoping that there would be better days ahead for us after the war, when she was a little more mature. And, don't forget, we had two beautiful kids.

The night before I was inducted we had a big going-away party at the club. It was a madhouse. You couldn't move. People were standing three-deep at the bar.

I played all night on the stage and June came up and sang a few songs. The party began to get really emotional. It was going to be real hard for me to leave this life and go into the army and who knows what.

For the last song of the night I called June on stage and sang it to her. It was a snappy polka tune called "Bye, Bye, My Baby."

We sang it cheerfully, devil-may-care. We didn't want it to be schmaltzy. When you combined it with the sentiment of the occasion, it had quite an effect. Everybody in the joint was crying, me included.

The next morning I left for Fort Knox, Kentucky, where I took basic training. After that they sent me to Camp Fannin, Texas. I was in the First Infantry Division. We were told we would eventually serve as replacements for soldiers coming back from the front.

I got along well with the guys in camp, and did my share of KP. I always skipped breakfast because that gave me an extra half hour of sleep every morning.

I had taken my accordion to camp with me and pretty soon I was entertaining the guys in the barracks. Then I was called to play at the Officers Club. I liked that because it got me out of KP. But it must have made somebody jealous. I became a victim of a prank.

In those days they'd inspect your bunk real close every morning. If your bed wasn't made up just right or if something was out of place they would put you on KP or take away your weekend pass. Well, one morning the sergeant was inspecting my bunk and he saw a cigaret butt under my bed. He put me on KP. I peeled potatoes for ten hours.

I didn't say anything, but when it happened again I went

to the sergeant and explained to him that I didn't even smoke. The sergeant read the riot act to the men and after that I didn't have any more trouble.

It was altogether different then in the army than it is today. We wanted to be good GIs and we felt we were doing what was best for the country.

We had no qualms about the war. Everybody was against Hitler and the Japanese. We all felt we were fighting to preserve freedom, and there was no second-guessing. We took the government's word for it. We didn't really understand what was going on, of course. But if we were told we had to fight we were ready to help out. There was no dissension. We all felt we lived in the greatest country on earth.

When our training was over they sent us home for a two-week furlough. They told us to have a good time, because when the furlough ended we were going to go overseas. Nobody had any idea where we were going, but I had a hunch it would be a long time before we saw the good old United States again.

While I was home, I figured we better make some more polka records while we had the chance. People were talking about the war lasting for ten years.

I got hold of Hokavar, the bass player, Naglitch, the pianist, and banjo player Joe Miklavic. We went to Fred Wolf's Cleveland Recording Studio again with Heinie Martin and cut the records on the Jolly label. The band went under the name of the Happy Slovenians. I paid for the entire production of the records.

Unbelievably, in one afternoon we cut 32 songs and 16 records. We had no time to fool around. If somebody hit a wrong note, we just kept going. One time one of the guys said we should record a song over He said there were too many clinkers in it. I said, "Leave the clinkers in. People like it better that way." In later years we were more careful. There was more competition.

By the time the records came out, of course, I was back in the army. So I put Wolf in charge of all the business transactions. We split 50-50 on the profits.

Those records were another instant hit. They sold so fast

the demand couldn't be filled. Unfortunately, there was a shellac shortage and it was hard to get enough records made. In fact, people who bought new records in those days were asked to bring in one or two of their old ones in exchange for the one they bought. The companies wanted the old records for the shellac. Finally, the shellac shortage got so bad that no more discs could be made. Wolf didn't know what to do.

Then a sharp guy came along. His name was Don Gabor and he represented Continental Records. He saw how well our records had sold in Cleveland and he had an idea they might move the same way all over the country. He offered to buy the rights to all the records, including the masters and the copyrights, for $3,000.

Wolf figured that he might as well sell them since he couldn't get anymore made anyway. He thought we were making a nice profit and that Gabor was a sucker.

But Gabor somehow was able to get more records produced. Later he took the same master records, dubbed in voices under different labels, and made all kinds of money. He had a virtual corner on the polka record market in the whole country. Nobody else was making any polka discs.

I didn't find out about any of this until the war ended and I got out of the army. When I saw what Wolf had done, I was furious. But what was the use? I had given him power of attorney to make any deals. Besides, it was too late to do anything about it.

But I didn't care about that then. I had the little matter of the war to worry about. The army shipped 25,000 of us to Scotland on the Queen Elizabeth. It wasn't a pleasure cruise. We were squeezed in like sardines. I slept in the bottom deck of the ship and my bunk was jammed up against the ceiling.

While we were in Scotland we got more training. They taught me to use a flamethrower. How did they pick me for that? I don't know. I just looked at the bulletin board one day and my name was on the list. You didn't ask questions. You just did it.

It was one of the most dangerous jobs in the army. You had to get close to your target, within 25 feet or so. You had to learn to go in low, on your belly, carrying the flamethrower.

It was a suicide job. Fortunately, I never actually had to use a flamethrower in combat. But I knew how to do it if it had been necessary.

While in Scotland we were also warned what to expect when we reached our next destination—England. Our officers told us we'd see a lot of black soldiers going around with white girls. The officers said they didn't want us making any trouble because of it. They said that the English girls thought the black Americans were Indians.

We sure did see a lot of that in England. I never saw any trouble develop over it, but that doesn't mean that I liked it. I couldn't see it then and I can't see it now. I believe that whites should live with whites and blacks with blacks.

Now don't go thinking I'm a racist, because I'm not. Back in Collinwood High School one of my best friends was black. His name was Dawson and I knew his whole family. You couldn't find a better guy.

I remember another black fellow from our old neighborhood. He hung around with Slovenes so much that he could sing in Slovenian. He could even peck out a few tunes on the cheesebox.

After a few weeks in England we were sent to France. That was in late 1944, and the Allies had already run the Germans out of France. Everything was bombed and the streets were all deserted. I remember St. Lo, France, was blown to bits. Not a brick was standing. We just walked through France, with no fighting. The French people were very nice to us. It looked like maybe I was going to have an easy war. Then came Aachen.

Aachen was the first German city to be taken by the Allies. The Germans fought there with all they had because it was on their homeland. It was a symbol. I got my first taste of action there.

The fighting was in close, street to street, house to house, room to room. The houses were close together and we'd go from one to the other, knocking down the walls of one to get into the next one. One day I opened up a door of a room and saw a young German soldier standing there. He was only about 18. We were both stunned. He turned and ran and I was too surprised to do anything about it.

The battle for Aachen went on for weeks. It was nip and tuck. One day the Allies would have the city and the next day the Germans would have it back.

One of the worst things was standing on sentry duty during the night. You couldn't see a thing, and it was dark and scary. Everything went through your mind. If you heard a squirrel run down a tree you were ready to shoot.

In December of 1944 Hitler launched his final offensive of the war. This was the Germans' last-ditch effort to win, and they poured a million men behind their strongest weapons at the Allied troops in Belgium and Germany. This was the struggle that came to be known in the history books as the Battle of the Bulge. I was right in the middle of it.

Everything was mass confusion. The drawing-board plans of the generals were forgotten. There was so much shooting, bombing, smoke and noise you couldn't tell half the time where your troops were and where the enemy was. You couldn't see anything. If somebody told you to shoot, you shot blindly, not knowing what you were shooting at. If somebody told you to run in a certain direction, you ran there, without knowing the reason why. You were always hiding, and you were always tired and cold and scared.

One night, in the middle of all this chaos, about a dozen of us found ourselves alone in the Hertgen Forest. The rest of our platoon had backed out and we didn't know it. We didn't know where we were, or what direction we should move in. So we just stayed together in a circle about the size of a room, hoping somebody would show up and tell us what to do.

Eventually, we fell asleep. It was ice cold and it snowed all night. In the morning we were covered by snow. I was so cold that I had to look at my hand to make sure it was there. I couldn't feel anything. We could see a big German force a few hundred yards away, but they didn't know we were there. We were cut off from everybody—no communications.

We couldn't get up to fight because the Germans would have slaughtered us. There were too many of them. But we knew if we had to stay there a long time we would freeze to death. We thought of surrendering, but there was talk that the Germans never took prisoners. Some of the boys despaired and began to cry.

Lucky for us, the momentum of the battle shifted and suddenly the Germans were gone. In a little while we were found by our troops. We were completely buried by the snow. We'd been there for about 24 hours.

If you want to know how we felt, sometime when it's zero outside go and sleep in the snow for 24 hours. You won't feel too good when you wake up. I could barely move.

They took us out on stretchers and flew us to a hospital in Paris. My hands and feet were frost-bitten and they felt as though they were burning. I was given some treatment and was supposed to rest.

But I didn't respond to that at all. My hands and feet hurt so much I was afraid to touch anything. Then both my hands and feet turned as black as paint. Gangrene had set in.

I was rushed to a hospital in Oxford, England, where they gave me penicillin every three hours around the clock. But I was still black up to my wrists and ankles. I was never so scared and sick in my life. I threw up just from the way my feet looked.

I had a tall, young doctor who was looking after me. He was a nice guy and I felt he was doing everything he could. But after a couple of days he told me he would have to amputate my hands and feet. He said it was the only way he could save my life.

He told me I didn't have any chance to survive otherwise, and said the gangrene would spread through my whole body. This was about a week after our rescue from the forest.

The doctor said there was no time to be lost. By this time I was so doped up that nothing hurt. My mind was made up. I figured it wasn't worth living without my hands and feet. I didn't have the guts to go back home that way and face my wife and children. I might have gone along with the doctor if he had said they'd take only one foot or one hand. But he didn't put it to me that way.

I made the decision. I refused to let him amputate. "All right," the doctor said, "but you're a dead duck." He wasn't saying that to be mean. He really felt that way.

That was the worst time of my life. I couldn't understand why this had to happen to me, especially to my hands. I was a musician. I needed my hands. Why couldn't I have just been shot in the back? I didn't really think that much about music, of course. I knew I was through as a musician. I was just hoping that maybe some day I'd be able to tie my shoes again.

They kept shooting the penicillin and drugs into me. I asked a nurse to write a letter home for me and ask them to send me a prayer book. She did it. I just lay still. Finally things began to turn my way. The discoloring started to go and then I knew I was going to make it.

I can't describe how great I felt when I saw the black start to fade. After an experience like that I knew I'd never let little things worry me again. And I had a new respect for that old axiom: Nothing is more important than good health.

The tall doctor and the whole staff came to see me. I was the talk of the ward. The doctor kept apologizing. I told him I didn't blame him. He was only trying to do what he thought was best.

The doctor gave me a rubber ball to squeeze to get some action in my hands. A few days later he said, "I understand you play the accordion. It would be good therapy for you to play. I'll get you one."

He brought me an old piano accordion, but I couldn't play anything at first. I was like a beginner again. It took a good month of practice before I could play like I wanted.

I healed almost 100 per cent, although you can see some of the effects of the frostbite and gangrene even today. A couple of my toes are curled under my feet. It looks as though they're missing. I just recently had them operated on to straighten them out, but it didn't work.

After I recovered, I started having some fun. I would go around the hospital wards and entertain the other wounded soldiers. I played popular wartime songs, like "Lili Marlene," and we'd all sing.

A lot of the soldiers were of English descent and couldn't care less about polkas, but I played some anyway. I knew that at first they would think they were cornball, but that they'd get to like them more than the standard popular songs. That's exactly what happened. Anytime you're around young guys, especially if they're GIs, you can't go wrong playing polkas.

When I left the hospital they assigned me to Special Services to entertain troops. I formed a hillbilly band. We had five men, a pianist, a fiddler, a bass man, a harmonica player and me. We were an act, a comical band. I dressed like a girl once in a while, just for laughs. We were in a series of acts called "Laugh Parade."

We were flown and driven behind the front all around Europe. One time we performed for General George (Old Blood and Guts) Patton and his famed Third Army.

We also had a bigger concert band and I played the accordion in that one too. We would do complete stage shows from camp to camp. The sergeant in charge of that show was Sidney Mills, whose uncle owned Mills Publishing Co. in New York, one of the biggest music publishing houses in the country. Sidney took a liking to me and told me to make sure I looked him up after the war. I did. Years later Mills Publishing put out all my songbooks, from which I still collect royalties.

We lived well and ate well in Special Services. I was at a dentist's office in Paris in April when the news came that President Roosevelt had died. We all felt bad. To millions of Americans who lived through the Depression, he was the greatest president we ever had.

When the war in Europe ended in May 1945, I was just outside Paris. We really put on a no-holds-barred show that night. Everybody went crazy. We all felt we had been lucky to survive the war, whereas a lot of other young guys hadn't.

I didn't get out of the army until the following December, however. I was supposed to be discharged on Christmas Eve, 1945, but all the officers went home for the holiday. A fellow soldier, Ross Vaccaro, who lived just outside Indiantown Gap, Pennsylvania, the separation center, took me to his house for Christmas. I was finally discharged on December 26, 1945.

Years later Vaccaro visited me when we were playing at the Village Barn in New York City. He had just become part of a singing group and he asked me for advice on how they could get started in the business. I told him to get a good manager and not be hasty in signing a contract. Then he sang a new tune the group had come up with. I told him it sounded good and that I thought it had a good chance. Ross thanked me and left. It wasn't long before that song became a million-selling record and propelled Ross and his group into nationwide popularity. The song was "Sin" and the group was The Four Aces, one of the great quartets of the 1950s.

My thoughts about war? Well, I'm not political-minded. I do my work and I figure the government has its job to do. I figure it knows what it's doing. I went in a private and came out a private. I did what I was told and didn't want anything else.

But I can't see people who don't even know each other killing each other. And yet, the soldier has no choice. If he doesn't kill them, they'll kill him. It has to make you bitter. I had nightmares for a year after I got home.

CHAPTER VII

JUST BECAUSE

I came back from the service and into the biggest boomtime I had ever known. The war was over after almost four years and the GIs who had fought it out on Guadalcanal and Normandy and Cassino were starving for fun. There was plenty of money around too. Every polka spot in Cleveland was jumping like crazy.

One of my best friends at that time was Johnny Pecon, the fine chromatic accordion player. I had become acquainted with Johnny before the war and after I came back we got really close. We were born in the same year, 1915, and we were like brothers.

When he wasn't playing with his band someplace, Johnny was almost always at our bar. Many were the times he'd come in with one of his band members like Church Srnick or Whitey Lovsin after he played a job somewhere. He'd play some more at our bar from the sheer joy of entertaining. Sometimes we'd jam all night and have such a good time we'd sleep in the bar. When Frank Spilar came in to open up at six in the morning we'd be hollering for service.

Johnny was a great all-around guy in those days. They don't make 'em like that anymore. People are more self-centered now. A tall, lanky guy, he was the champion sport. He bought drinks for everybody. Whatever he made, he threw back across the bar. And he would play for anybody, at any time. He'd keep his accordion in his car, or he'd walk into a bar with it, and if somebody asked him to strike up a tune he was always ready. When he played it was with everything he had, whether he was playing in a packed hall or for a few cronies at the bar.

Everybody knows how good he was with that box. He had a style all his own, a peculiarly sentimental, sophisticated blending of Slovenian and American music, and he had perfect pitch and tempo. He was also one of the first polka musicians to include pop music regularly in his repertoire. He established the pattern that most polka bands still follow today, playing three polkas, three waltzes and three modern tunes.

My dad took a terrific liking to Johnny. To tell you the truth, I think he liked him better than he liked me. That's what people used to say around our bar anyway. It never bothered me. It made me feel good to see my dad and my best buddy get along that well.

Johnny would come into the bar in the afternoon and my dad would be waiting for him. They'd drink and tell jokes in Slovenian and pretty soon everybody in the bar would be laughing. Then they'd go out together and make the rounds of a few more bars.

But it wasn't all like that. Anybody who remembers him will tell you that Johnny was a serious musician. We were always talking about how to make this song sound better, or how to change this tempo, things like that.

Johnny loved to make people happy and he had an artist's sense of the dramatic. A good example of that occurred during the war. Johnny was in the Seabees and he came home on furlough.

He didn't tell anybody except his family that he was coming home. He wanted it to be a surprise. Then he called John (Hokey) Hokavar, the bass player, and asked him to meet him at the St. Vitus School Hall in the old St. Clair neighborhood. They were having some kind of big doing there on a holiday afternoon.

The flabbergasted Hokavar agreed and also brought along guitarist Mickey Kling, as Pecon had specified. The three of them met in the St. Vitus school basement.

"I don't want anybody to know I'm here," Pecon explained. The war had been going on for about three years and Pecon had been away almost all that time.

"I learned a good new song in the Seabees," Pecon told Hokavar and Kling. "It's called 'Just Because,' and we ought to sing it here today." Pecon sang the song to them and they memorized it right away.

Then they went on the stage, behind the closed curtain. Johnny had made arrangements with the priests. Suddenly, in the middle of the banquet, the curtain opened. The people in the hall immediately recognized Johnny, sitting there in his sailor uniform. They gave him an ovation. Johnny was well known, of course, for he had a good polka band for years before the war.

Johnny and his little group warmed up the crowd with some good polkas and then they played and sang, "Just Because." It was the first time the song had been sung by a polka band in Cleveland. The crowd wouldn't let them quit. They made them play it over and over.

Then somebody started a grand march with Pecon, Hokavar and Kling at the head of the parade. Johnny led the people outside, like a pied piper, and everybody marched around the school, singing "Just Because."

Flushed with this triumph, Pecon, Hokavar and Kling started making the rounds. Eddie Habat still likes to tell how he was playing in my bar that night and how he heard that Pecon was home and that he was visiting every polka spot in town. The word was out that he was heading for my bar. I was in the army then, of course.

Sure enough, it happened. The people in my bar could hear Pecon, Hokey and Kling playing as they got out of their car. They were still singing as they walked into my bar, "Just because you think you're so pretty . . ." Johnny couldn't buy a drink that night.

I didn't hear "Just Because" until much later, after I got home from the army. In 1946, I started again with my old four-piece band, with Hokey slapping the bass fiddle, Naglitch on piano and Georgie Cook on banjo. After Pecon and I became close, he joined us too, and we finally developed the new sound I had been looking for.

As I said before, I had never liked a saxophone in my band, and I had stopped using one back in the late 1930s. I experimented with other instruments and finally decided on the solovox, which was kind of an electric organ. You could only play one note on it at a time, no chords. We used the solovox as far back as 1943, when we made those 32 records in one day.

But one solovox wasn't quite the answer either. The sound wasn't full enough. So I tried two solovoxes. That produced the sound I wanted, and we stayed with it. Naglitch and I would harmonize on the solovoxes on parts of songs, with me playing the melody. Pecon would add more harmony with his chromatic accordion. Then I'd come back in with more melody on my accordion. It was a sound that polka bands have been copying ever since.

By the way, when Johnny joined me it was another first. Nobody had ever used two accordions in one polka band before. There had been one or two accordion teams who played together, like Kozel and Schmidt, but they played alone. They weren't with a full band.

I also went into business with Pecon about that time. We bought the Metropole Bar on East 55th Street and St. Clair in 1946. Lou Trebar, another accomplished accordionist, and Sam Slapic were also in on the deal. Slapic had been helping my family run our bar during the war.

We bought the Metropole from Joe Vidmar for $40,000. I put up all the money, with the agreement that the other fellows would pay me back. The plan was to have Pecon and Trebar alternating on stage and working behind the bar with Slapic. They were each supposed to play for one hour, then tend bar for one hour. Johnny couldn't always do this, of course. We were beginning to travel more and more, especially after I signed a contract with Columbia Records.

Columbia figured that the more we traveled, the better we would become known, and the more records we would sell. Our contract with Columbia called for us to make four records (eight sides) a year. The contract had two-year options and Columbia kept picking it up for 26 years.

I also brought Pecon in with me in my songbook publishing business. Joe Trolli, my old accordion teacher, Pecon and I would take old Slovene folk tunes that had been around for hundreds of years, put new piano and accordion arrangements to them, and add American titles. That was when my friendship with my old army sergeant, Mills, came in handy.

I called him with the idea and Mills Publishing Co. put out our songbooks. They would include twelve songs in each one, with my name and picture on the cover. The books sold for $1 apiece, and I got 50% of the royalties, with Johnny getting 35% and Trolli 15%. I got the 50% because without me there would have been no deal with Mills Music.

We put out seven of those books, and then when Pecon left, Trolli and I wrote seven more. I gave Trolli 50% of the royalties after Pecon split.

The books are still selling today for $1.50 each. Teachers like them because we simplified the music so students could play.

When we worked, we would take a bottle of whiskey off the shelf in my bar. Then Pecon, Trolli and I would go into the basement of the bar and start writing.

Johnny would fool around on the accordion and if he came up with something new Trolli would write the notes down on paper. Johnny had the gift of melody but he couldn't read music then. I couldn't spend as much time down there as they did because I was still running the bar.

A lot of good songs came out of that basement. One of them was inspired by my dad. He came downstairs one afternoon while Trolli and Pecon were pecking away and said, "Hey, boys, why don't you write a song about me?"

Pecon and Trolli thought it was a good idea. While they drank and laughed with my dad, they invented a tune called "Andy's Jolly Hop." It was one of our best numbers and we still play it today.

I'm not pretending all of our songs were original. One of our biggest sellers was the "Tick Tock Polka." Trolli lifted it from an old Italian folk song.

Trolli found another good one from one of his accordion pupils. This guy was about 35 years old and he invited Trolli to his house for his grandmother's 80th birthday party. During the party, the grandmother sang an old German song. It caught Trolli's ear and he took it and put a Slovenian style second part to it. It turned out to be the "Rosalinda Waltz," another classic.

The first time I ever heard "Just Because" was in my bar. Trolli was playing there and Pecon came in and asked if he could join him onstage, just for the fun of it. Joe said, "Sure," and Pecon got his box.

"Here's a good number we played in the Seabees," said Johnny, and he started singing and playing the song. I liked the simplicity of the lyrics right away. I knew people would be able to learn the words fast and that was always good. The simpler the words, the better. That's why songs such as "Beer Barrel Polka" and Bobby Vinton's "My Melody of Love" catch on. They just have a few words and a lot of la la la's.

Anyway, as soon as I heard "Just Because" I asked Pecon where he got it. He said he'd learned it from the Sheldon Brothers, whom he'd known in the Seabees. The Sheldon Brothers had written the song before the war and recorded it as a hillbilly tune. But it hadn't succeeded.

I felt the song had potential as a polka and I said to Trolli and Pecon, "We want a second part for that." Down to the basement they went.

Pecon said to Trolli, "Joe, you got a good second part?" Trolli said he did and played an old Italian bit. Johnny didn't dig it and said, "No, not quite like that. Like this." He gave it a Slovenian touch and that was how it stayed.

Everybody liked the song. It became part of our standard repertoire. People asked us to play it two or three times a night everywhere we went.

We picked up another good song in 1947. It was called the "Rendezvous Waltz," and it was a landmark song for us because it was the first vocal we ever recorded.

It's funny how you get some of your best songs. This one came from a woman who was a friend of ours and who never wrote a song before or since in her life.

Her name was Mary Luzar and she and her husband owned the Rendezvous Bar on West 25th Street in Cleveland. Eddie Stampfl, the accordion player, used to hang out there. One day, when me and the Yanks were heading for Chicago, we stopped at the bar for a little afternoon fun.

We were playing and drinking and Mary said to us, "Why don't you write a song in honor of the Rendezvous Bar?" We thought that was a good idea.

Me and Pecon and Naglitch and the others started fooling

around with some notes and pretty soon, fortified by a little booze, we had a nice melody. There were a lot of people in the bar and they all said they liked it.

Then Mary said the song needed words. She got a pencil. With a little help from the boys, she wrote the lyrics at the bar. The next day we recorded the song in the Wrigley Building in Chicago and it sold about 50,000 records. That was about standard for us in that era. We never dreamed of making a million-seller.

Columbia wasn't too happy about us recording "Rendezvous Waltz" with the lyrics, by the way. The company wasn't sure that the lyrics were original. They sounded too professional. Columbia didn't want to get involved in paying royalties to some lyricist who turned up down the line.

So we had to record the song twice, once without the lyrics and once with the lyrics. All the Yanks joined in on the singing. When Columbia was sure the words were ours, they released the record with the words. From then on most of our records were vocals.

Late in 1947 Columbia gave us a rush call to come to New York. The Musicians Union was threatening to go on strike when its contract was up at the end of the year. Columbia wanted us to come in and record some records so they'd have them on hand if the musicians did go out.

On the afternoon of New Year's Eve, 1947, me and the boys went to the studio. With me were Pecon, Hokavar, Cook, Naglitch and Whitey Lovsin on drums. A word about them:

Naglitch, the pianist, was with my bands from the start, longer than almost any musician I ever had. Al was a superb pianist, out of this world. He might have known more about music than the rest of us put together. He walked with a limp as the result of a leg ailment. After he left the music business he dropped out of sight for years. Just recently I found out he is now in the Lake County Home in Painesville, Ohio. Lovsin was the pretty boy of our band, one of the handsomest guys you ever saw. He pursued good times relentlessly, as most Slovene musicians did, and died when he was only about 40. Hokavar was a good singer and showman. He had a carefree way of slapping the bass fiddle that made him extremely popular with audiences. He once won the Ohio weightlifting championship. A 193-pounder, he picked up 350 pounds. There is no need to say much about Cook. He is one of the all-time banjo greats in the polka field. He still plays around Cleveland.

The record session went well that New Year's Eve. Columbia gave us three hours to make four sides. We completed the songs Columbia wanted, and had a few minutes left over to make one more record.

We put "That Night in May" on one side. We had room for one more song. I told the Columbia representative who was present that we ought to put "Just Because" on the other side.

Usually Columbia paid attention to my judgment, but this time the man said no. "Why go again with that turkey?" he said. "The Sheldon Brothers recorded it and it didn't work. Let's try something else."

I argued with him. I told him this was the song that was most requested by our audiences. But he wouldn't listen. We started yelling at each other. I threw some sheet music on the floor and kicked a chair across the room. But no matter how I argued, I couldn't get through to this guy.

Finally I said to him, "All right, I'll make a deal with you. If you let us record this song I'll buy the first 10,000 records myself." I knew I could sell them.

That convinced him. Columbia wasn't taking the chance anymore. I was. He gave us the go-ahead. We only had time to play the song once though. Our three hours were almost up. I told the boys to play it as perfect as possible. We wouldn't get a second chance if we fouled up.

We quieted down and played "Just Because" without a rehearsal, with Pecon and me harmonizing on the vocal.

We didn't know it then, but we were making polka and recording history.

CHAPTER VIII

JOHNNY PECON

Our recording of "Just Because" took off like a skyrocket. We got our biggest boost in Boston, where, to my knowledge, nobody ever cared about polka music before.

For some reason, Columbia concentrated its early promotion of the record there. I guess it felt Beantown was ready for a good polka.

Columbia tried out the song in a moderately active retail store in Boston. The dealer played the song for the first twenty-six people who walked in. Twenty-five of them bought the record.

Then Columbia took the record to WHDH Radio's Bob Clayton, who was one of the leading disc jockeys in Boston. Clayton was talked into playing it.

Within two minutes after he played it, the station switchboard lit up like a Christmas tree. More than 60 phone calls came in requesting the record to be played again. Clayton repeated the record within ten minutes and it was played on WHDH six more times that evening.

Columbia realized it had a potential hit on its hands and started promoting it as much as it could. The company put up a huge 45-foot sign at its headquarters. It was the biggest flash poster ever designed for the promotion of a record. It read, "LISTEN TO THE SENSATIONAL "JUST BECAUSE" BY FRANKIE YANKOVIC AND HIS YANKS ON COLUMBIA RECORDS." During the first week 25,000 copies of the record were sold in Boston.

That spectacular showing was repeated in cities all over the country. In Albany, New York, for example, a salesman named Bill Stillwell took the record to wholesale stores one morning and in one day sold 1,725 copies. The records were all bought after one demonstration. It wasn't long before "Just Because" sold a million copies.

The band became famous, but I never did cash in on that song the way I should have. If I knew then what I know now I would have made money galore.

I had a hot band. Everybody wanted us. I was happy to be so much in demand, but I only charged my usual rate. I should have tripled my price, or taken a percentage of the gate. People were flocking into ballrooms to see us. We were collecting $300 or $500 a night, while the ballroom operators were making $10,000.

For instance, we drew a crowd of 8,000 at the Million Dollar Ballroom in Milwaukee. That was the all-time record there. After we left, the Guy Lombardo band came in and the ballroom owner, George Devine, told Guy: "You think you can draw a crowd. Listen, I got a little five-piece band that can outdraw all you guys." He was talking about us, of course.

I regret that I didn't have an agent then. We could have been booked into every top night club in the country and racked up all kinds of money.

But I can't really blame myself. After all, I was just a Slovene from Collinwood, one generation removed from the boat, and so were the rest of the Yanks. We were spinach green.

In 1949, lightning struck again with "The Blue Skirt Waltz." We were playing at Ciro's Night Club in Philadelphia when I got a call from Jack Mills of Mills Publishing. He said he'd bought a whole catalogue of Bohemian songs and he wanted to send me the sheet music to see if I liked any of them.

I went through all the songs, but there was only one that caught my interest. It was called 'The Red Skirt Waltz." I called Mills in New York and told him that I felt the song needed lyrics.

Mills said that was no problem. He said that he had the best lyricist in the business on his staff. His name was Mitchell Parish and he had written the words to numerous popular songs, including the classic "Stardust."

In no time at all Parish came up with the lyrics and changed the title of the song to "The Blue Skirt Waltz." Then I suggested to Columbia that it might be a good idea to get a couple of female vocalists for the record. I felt it was the kind of song that could use girls' voices.

So Columbia hired two girls from New York, the Marlin Sisters, who had been singing Jewish songs in Brooklyn and Manhattan. They had never sung any polka tunes before.

Before we went to New York to record, we made a side trip to Strabane, Pennsylvania, to see an old friend, Frank Tomsic. He owned a car agency in Strabane and was also very active in Slovene affairs. When we got to his house we went into his back yard and rehearsed "Blue Skirt." Tomsic wanted us to play outside so that all his friends could hear. I guess he wanted to show us off a little. From what we could tell, the people of Strabane liked the song a lot.

When we reached the studio in New York, the Marlin Sisters were already there. We had never seen or heard of them before. I just assumed that Columbia had hired some singers with good voices. They were nice, pleasant girls, but we didn't get much of a chance to get to know them or even talk to them. I never even learned their first names.

It was all business. We worked out an arrangement with the sisters singing a duet on the verse and Pecon and I singing on the chorus. Cook, Naglitch, and Stan Slejko, one of Cleveland's finest bass players, backed us up. Slejko was filling in for Hokavar, for some reason. I can't recall why. Hokey never did like to travel much, though.

Then we cut the other side, a polka called, "Charley was a Boxer," with the Marlin Sisters singing the Mitchell Parish lyrics again. Then the girls smiled, said goodbye and disappeared from our lives forever. It's amazing. They sang on one of the most popular polka records ever made and that was the only time I ever saw them.

I don't know what happened to them. I do have one picture of them, which was taken at the studio. I'd sure like to hear from them if they're still around.

Our experience with "Blue Skirt" was complicated by the fact that soon after we made the record Naglitch left the

Yankovic's Bar band, 1946 (left to right): Mickey Kling, Pete Sokach, Kenny Bass, Eddie Habat, Frank Yankovic, John (Hokey) Hokavar, Jim Kozel, and Johnny Pecon.

The Polka King at his peak, around 1950.

Yankovic with one of his great early bands, 1949. Clockwise, from above right: Johnny Pecon, accordion; Al Naglitch, piano; Georgie Cook, banjo; and Church Srnick, bass.

Yankovic with his most versatile band, 1955. Rear, from left: Carl Paradiso, banjo; Tops Cardone, accordion. Front, from left: Al Leslie, bass; Frank Yankovic, accordion; and Buddy Griebel, piano.

For years Yankovic traveled in this 1937 bus, which he bought in 1959. He is shown here in Denver with Mr. and Mrs. Wayne Motley and accordionist Herb Eberle, right.

Another top Yankovic band in the 1960s. Clockwise, from bottom: Ray Smolik, piano; Pete Rogan, bass; Roger DiBenedict. banjo; Mike Zitkovich, accordion; and Frankie Yankovic, accordion.

band. He had been with me for a long time and was tired of the traveling.

Naglitch went back to Cleveland and hooked up with the Tune Mixers, a fine band featuring Eddie Habat and Pete Sokach on the accordions. This band, which played almost exclusively around Ohio, also had Kenny Bass on the bass fiddle, Al Tercek on drums and Todd Roberts on banjo.

Soon after Naglitch joined them, the Tune Mixers had a recording date with Decca. Bass' sister, who played the piano, had come across an old, forgotten piece of sheet music in her house. It was "The Red Skirt Waltz," and she liked it. She recommended that the Tune Mixers record it, and they planned to do so.

At the recording studio, Naglitch immediately recognized the song as "The Blue Skirt Waltz," and told his new band he had just recorded it with me a few weeks before.

When they found that out, Sokach, Habat and Bass decided to try to beat us to the punch. They recorded their own version of the song, complete with Parish's lyrics, and hustled it out. It was in the stores while ours was still on ice.

This was all legitimate, by the way. Everything is fair in love and music competition. I did the same thing years later with "Who Stole the Kishka?" The Maty Brothers from Chester, Pennsylvania, had put out the disc and when it started to hit the charts, Columbia rushed me to New York. I was told to come alone, so I used Columbia's staff band on the record. It was the only record I ever cut in which a saxophone was used. "Who Stole the Kishka?" was a good seller for us, by the way.

The Tune Mixers made out very well with "Blue Skirt Waltz" too. Bass claims the record sold 700,000. I doubt that, but I know it moved well.

When the Tune Mixers came out with their version, Columbia got moving and put out our record. Despite our late start, we caught and passed Decca and the song became our second million-seller.

Even today, we get more requests for "Just Because" and "Blue Skirt" than any other songs. We have to play both on every job. I never get tired of playing them either. Of the two, "Blue Skirt" is the more popular, without a doubt.

We never made another million-seller and, to tell you the truth, I don't really understand why. I feel that I've made records that were better than those two, or at least just as good. I'm talking about songs such as "Charm of Your Beautiful Dark Eyes," "Beloved Be Faithful," and "Blue Eyes Crying in the Rain." But you never can tell what the public will go for.

Much of any record's success depends on the promotion. You can have a great record, but if you can't convince the record company to give it that big promotional push it won't get anywhere.

Polka record sales are down all over the country. A lot of artists sell only about 1,000 copies today. One big reason for that, I think, is that there are too many polka bands getting into the act.

When we struck gold, there were only a few polka bands making records, and the major record companies such as Capital, Decca, Columbia and RCA financed the discs.

But today, a young band gets started, puts up a few thousand dollars of its own money, and makes its own record. I can't blame them for doing that, because it gives them the exposure they need. I did it myself when I started. The difference is that when I cut my first records, the public asked me to do it, and there was nobody else making polka records. There must be hundreds of bands and singers doing that now.

The end result is that nobody gets a really big record anymore. The polka business is better than ever, but too many people are cutting up the pie. That's why the big record firms are no longer interested in picking up the tab.

The biggest polka album made in recent years was Father Frank Perkovich's "Polka Mass," in which religious lyrics were set to old Slovene folk tunes. I understand the Minnesota priest sold about 50,000 copies of "Polka Mass" in the last couple of years.

I sold about the same number when I made "Beers and Cheers," with Frank Novak on the button box a few years back. That album, by the way, may have started the button box craze that's around now. I remembered Novak from the old days. He was an executive in a factory in Cleveland and had seldom played professionally. But I heard him at a party and suggested we rejuvenate the old button box and cut a record. It worked so well that Novak has cut several more on his own. It also gave him a second career. Since his retirement from the factory, he has come into demand as a button box teacher. He now has dozens of pupils and is busier now than he was before he retired.

It was after "Just Because" and "Blue Skirt" that my troubles really began. They were caused, of course, by money. That, plus the fact that familiarity breeds contempt.

The boys in the band started getting the idea that I was making too much money. They felt they deserved just as much as I did. They weren't satisfied anymore with the standard side men's fees they had been getting.

I blame myself for that. I should have known that if I lived with them day after day, night after night, that sooner or later they would become jealous.

I stayed in the same hotels with the boys and I treated them just like I treated myself. I made the mistake of getting too close to them, and letting them get too close to me. When they get like that, they know too much of your business.

I should have treated them as though they were my children, not my brothers. Not that I was better than they were, but because that was the only way I could have managed them. When your side men feel they know you inside out, they start to grumble and start making demands and dictating.

The problem centered around the two guys who were closest to me—Pecon and Cook. Cook, the banjo player, was a smart little guy. He used to double as my business manager, handling a lot of the book work and setting up dates. On the few occasions when I was away, he was in charge of the band.

I already explained how thick I was with Pecon. But we had run into personal difficulties. Our venture together at the Metropole Bar hadn't worked out. Business was terrific at first, but then it fell off for a combination of reasons.

First, Johnny wasn't available to play there much anymore because he was on the road with me most of the time. Second, a new owner bought the building the bar was in and raised our rent. Third, a beer shortage hit in late 1947, and the Metropole never really recovered.

On slow nights, Trebar, who was in charge, would get bored and close up. He would go down the street to Tino Modic's bar and play his accordion there for nothing, entertaining the customers and drawing a crowd. When Pecon was at home, he'd do the same thing. Tino was our friend but he was our competitor too.

We finally decided to sell the Metropole for a loss. Since I had put up all the money, the other partners had to pay me their share of the deficit.

This financial setback must have bothered Johnny, especially when those two records hit big. I think people must have bugged him, talking about the money they guessed I must have made. It must have worked on Johnny's mind. He probably began brooding that he was on those records with me, traveling with me, living just the same as me. Yet he had nothing to show for it.

All I know is that Pecon began to complain about everything. Nothing was right anymore. The trips were too long, the hotels were lousy, I drove too fast, and all that kind of stuff. Cook joined in on the griping. We were snapping at each other all the time.

I tried to talk things over with Johnny more than once. I told him there was nothing we couldn't discuss. If he felt I was doing something wrong, I wanted him to tell me. I felt it was foolish to be mad about something silly, especially if it was money. I couldn't see a friendship like we had splitting up because of money or people's talk. But Johnny would never come out with it and tell me what was bothering him.

Things kept getting worse. Johnny was drinking too much. He wasn't himself on the bandstand anymore, and even his greatest admirers will admit that Johnny was never a showman. He was a wonderful accordionist, but he just didn't have much stage presence. He concentrated so hard on his playing that he neglected his showmanship.

This was important. I mean, we weren't playing in bars on St. Clair. The people who came to see us didn't just come to hear oom-pa-pa music. They came to see us put on a floor show too. A side man, even if he could play as well as Pecon, had to be a performer too.

By the time we got to the Village Barn in New York in 1949, I had just about had it. Johnny, who always had a gaunt face, looked completely run down. His general health was taking a beating. His performances at the Village Barn just weren't up to par. The manager asked me what was wrong with Pecon and suggested I do something to straighten him out.

Johnny and I were staying in the same room at the President's Hotel on Eighth Avenue when I decided to have it out with him. There was no argument. We just discussed everything. Finally, I said, "Johnny, it doesn't seem to be working out anymore. Maybe you don't want to stay with the band."

He agreed and said that it was bugging him to be on the road as much as we were. He said he would rather quit and go back to Cleveland, which he did. By this time, I had brought him in with me to entertain in my bar on East 152nd. We split as friends. He even asked me if I had somebody in mind to take his place with the band. He didn't want to leave me flat.

Then we ran into another financial problem and on November 14, 1949 Pecon filed for bankruptcy. The court ruled that he owed me $13,800. Johnny had to forfeit his share of the royalties from the songbooks we had put out. After that Mills Publishing sent me Johnny's share of the royalties.

Pecon then joined Lou Trebar and they formed their highly successful polka band. The outfit featured Srnick and Lovsin, along with Eddie Platt on the sax and Johnny Kafer on the piano. They were a fun-loving group and enjoyed life to the hilt. Trebar and Platt are the only ones still alive. Kafer, Lovsin and Srnick all died in middle age.

In the early 1950s, the doctors told Pecon that he had diabetes and that he would have to quit drinking entirely. Johnny, who had just gotten married, quit. He never took another drink. It takes a strong man to do that.

Pecon and Trebar teamed on classic polka records for Capital for many years. Johnny was justly inducted into the Polka Hall of Fame after his death from cancer in 1975. Five days before he died, 3,000 polka fans and 26 bands turned out in a massive tribute and benefit for Johnny at Slovenian Society Home in Euclid. He was truly a beloved musician.

The saddest thing about this whole episode is that Pecon and I never exchanged another word after we split. He snubbed me many times. I'd walk up to him with my hand outstretched and he'd never even look at me. It was the same way on the few occasions we shared the bandstand.

I could never see holding a grudge. Life is too short. We all make mistakes. How many times I tried to tell Johnny that if we could just talk things out we could be friends again. But I couldn't get anywhere with him. The same is true of Georgie Cook.

I thought for sure that Johnny would come to the wake when my dad died in 1949. They had been so close. But Johnny never showed up. Let him rest in peace, but I can't forgive him for that.

I was in Wisconsin when I got word that dad was sick. I hired a private plane and rushed home. When I saw how he looked, I couldn't get over it. I passed out in his bedroom. I'm real tough, but that really hit me.

That night I had a playing date in Chicago, a big lodge celebration for the SNPJ Pioneers. My dad had done a lot of work for SNPJ, and I knew he'd want me to play. So I flew back to Chicago for the job. But I came back to Cleveland almost every day until dad died.

When he passed away at the age of 69, Zele's Funeral Home handled the arrangements. Mr. Zele was an old friend of dad's and he flew back from a Florida vacation to direct everything. In fact, we delayed the wake a day on Mr. Zele's orders. He wanted time to get back from Florida to make sure that everything was just right.

On the final night of the wake, I played some of my dad's favorite Slovene songs before the hushed crowd in the funeral home. My mother and sisters wanted me to do it. It was a heck of a moment. I can still feel it.

I played strictly folk songs, no polkas or waltzes. When I played "Gor Cez Jezero," (Beyond the Lake) my dad's favorite, a lot of people cried. My nieces, Dorothy and Rose Kravos, who had recorded with me when they were little girls years before, also sang songs my dad liked.

It was the biggest funeral Zele's ever had. We had five flower cars alone.

I'll always feel, by the way, that dad died ahead of his time. He was feeling good but he was always afraid to die, so he went to a doctor for a checkup. The doctor told him he had cirrhosis of the liver and made dad quit drinking entirely. From then on dad's health went down fast. I think it was too much of a shock to his system to make him quit like that after all those years of steady imbibing. He wasn't a heavy drinker, just moderate, like a lot of Slovenes. I'm convinced he would have lived another ten years if the doctor hadn't made him quit.

Years later, when Pecon's mother died, I went to her wake. I felt Johnny couldn't refuse to talk to me then. I went to the funeral home every day of the wake, but he still wouldn't talk to me. I felt bad about it. I still do.

It's been charged that I got even with Pecon by using my influence to keep him off the Polka Varieties TV show, which runs every Sunday in Cleveland. But that's untrue. Johnny was frozen out of the show the last few years he was alive because of an argument he had with the producer. Cook hasn't talked to me for 20 years, but he appears regularly on the show.

When Johnny was dying in 1975 I wanted to see him in the hospital where he spent the better part of four months. But I felt it would do him more harm than good if I showed up. So I stayed away. When he died, Joey Miskulin and I sent a beautiful bouquet to the funeral home. Joey got a thank-you card. I didn't.

Pecon and Cook spread the word that I had promised to give them a piece of the profits from "Just Because" and "Blue Skirt" and that they quit me when I reneged.

But that's just not true. Think about it for a minute. Why would they ask for a piece of the profits on just those two records, when they never asked for a percentage of the profits from any of the other records we made, like "Rendezvous Waltz" or "Silk Umbrella." They had no way of knowing beforehand which would be the big hit.

I never had a co-op band, where we all shared equally in the profits. Pecon and Cook were paid strictly as side men. Further, they were paid the same whether the record was a flop or a hit.

Pecon might have thought he was entitled to more money from "Just Because" because he introduced me to the song. If so, he never told me that. I wouldn't buy that anyway. First, he didn't write it. The Sheldon brothers did. And, if it hadn't been for the fact that I was under contract to a major recording company, and believed in the song, "Just Because" might never have gotten past St. Clair Avenue.

Pecon also told people in later years that I offered him $1,000 to stay with the band. That's not true either. Maybe Johnny was referring to the fact when my royalty checks came in I would often give him $300 or $500 as a bonus. I didn't have to do it. I did it because I felt he deserved it.

The funny thing about the whole business is that I never made that much money on "Just Because." The disc sold for only 75 cents, and I got 5% of that. That's less than four cents a record. I'd say that altogether I made only about $50,000.

The Sheldon brothers probably made at least as much on it as I did, and didn't have any of the problems.

I've also heard the charge that I bought my house in South Euclid, a Cleveland suburb, with my first royalty check from "Just Because." But that's baloney too.

I bought the house in 1948 for $31,500, but I only put down $5,000. Equity Savings and Loan gave me a $26,000 loan for the rest. The house was a lot smaller then. We added a lot of rooms since. It's worth a lot more now.

The biggest royalty check I ever got from Columbia was for about $26,000. But that included royalties on "Just Because" and a lot of other songs.

As a matter of fact, aside from the personal satisfaction I got out of "Just Because," the main thing the song did for me was to give me enough money to keep me from going to jail.

You see, I had gotten into income tax trouble, and it wasn't even my fault. It went back to the years when I was in the army, when I had other people running the bar.

In 1950, out of a clear blue sky, I got word that Uncle Sam was investigating me for fraud. The investigator told me that he felt sorry for me. "You were in the army and weren't running the business, but the license is in your name and we have to come after you," he said.

The government had been checking the tavern books, which showed a discrepancy between the amount of whiskey sold and the amount of tax paid. The way Uncle Sam figured, my bar earned a lot more money than was declared. Where the money went, I don't know.

I fought the case in court and I won. I was cleared of fraud. But I still had to pay $37,000 in back taxes, $14,000 in interest, and $7,000 more in lawyers' fees.

That's a total of $58,000, more than I realized from "Just Because". Still, if I hadn't had the money from the record I might have had to go to jail.

It's a shame that Pecon and I wound up the way we did. No matter how hard they try, nobody will be able to match that certain sound we had. His chromatic accordion and my piano accordion blended in a unique way. So did our voices. The old records we made sound better than the new.

CHAPTER IX

LONG, LONG TRAIL

After the Pecon bunch left me, I couldn't just fold up and die. There was a whole world of polka fans out there and we were in demand. Well-meaning friends suggested that I take a few weeks off to reorganize the band, but I couldn't see that. It would have meant cancelling bookings and disappointing a lot of people around the country who wanted to see me and the Yanks. I decided to just keep traveling and trying out new players until I found a group that was compatible. I figured there was only one guy who was indispensable to the Yankovic band – me. After all, when I played in a town like Yankton, South Dakota, or Salt Lake City, Utah, the people didn't know or care if Pecon was a banjo player or if Cook played the accordion. The only one they knew was me.

My first job was to find an accordion player. I had a good one in Jimmy Kozel, a Clevelander, who came with me on a short trip through the Midwest. But Jimmy was a college student studying architecture and he couldn't stay with me year-round. So I kept looking.

It wasn't long before I found four men who eventually made up what I consider my best all-around band. I'm talking about Tops Cardone on accordion, Al Leslie, bass, Buddy Griebel, piano and solovox, and Carl Paradiso, guitar and banjo. Paradiso, by the way, was completely bald, so I bought him a $125 toupee. I didn't think it looked right for a young guy in show business to look like a cueball.

These fellows, all from the Greater Cleveland area, were professional musicians. Their background was in popular music, and they hadn't played polkas before. But good musicians can play anything. Paradiso, in fact, had never played a banjo, but he caught on real fast.

With these men, you never had to worry about them hitting a wrong note or not being able to read music. Not only that, they developed terrific arrangements. They were so versatile and talented, that I was able to go into other fields. With an outfit like that I was able to get to places like Hollywood and Las Vegas a lot easier.

We got some terrific press notices in those days. Billboard Magazine said this about us in 1949: "There's many a surprise in store for a first-time hearer and viewer of the Yankovic orchestra's work. The disk work sounds much fuller than the five pieces would normally sound. Quintet is a great international-styled group and can handle any type of request. Pianist Griebel has a touch on pops and standards that gives the band a society sound. Orchestra treats "The Hucklebuck" and "One O'Clock Jump" with enough bop to suit the goateed set. Band members deliver every number with gusto and their enthusiasm easily transmits to the dancers. Yankovic handles the vocals, with most of the numbers carrying special lyrics if the crowd is predominantly German, Polish or Bohemian. All sidemen either deliver solo work or join Yankovic on the lyrics. Leader and men are extremely hard workers and allow customers to come on stage for autographs at the short intermissions."

In 1950 Time Magazine said: "On the polka circuit nobody has to be told about Yankovic. His band has been known to outdraw name bands such as Vaughn Monroe by 2 to 1. Frankie makes music that sounds good to a lot of people who would not have listened twice to old-style polka bands with their hard-blowing brass and woodwinds and their um-pa-pa beat."

That same year Redbook Magazine wrote: "Frankie is a personable young man whose Columbia recording of "The Blue Skirt Waltz" last year was second in sales only to "Rudolph the Red-Nosed Reindeer," by Gene Autry. Inasmuch as the Yankovic band plays one-nighters almost exclusively, and to vast crowds, its profit is probably bigger than that of any ensemble in show business. Musically, it also has its points. The most important of these is its terrific beat, which is chiefly attributable to its banjoist, who is in a class with the men who played the instrument with some of the great jazz bands of other years. Indeed, this beat may be the principal reason why none of the hundreds of imitators of the Yankovic style has ever been able to approach its popularity."

The banjo player who got that terrific compliment was Cook, who was still with me in 1950.

As far as showmanship was concerned, the group revolved around Cardone. When I first asked him to come along for a tryout, he said he wasn't sure if he could handle the traveling. I suggested he come with me on a nine-day trip to the Milwaukee area to see how it went. I paid him $500 for the trial, which was big money.

Tops was impressed with the fine treatment we received. It opened his eyes. People picked up our dinner tabs, bought us gifts, and treated us like princes. Tops enjoyed it so much he stayed with me for six years.

Tops knew his obligations. He felt he had to go on the road to support his family in good style. He was talented and sold himself with a million-dollar smile. He wasn't as good a polka player as Pecon or, later, Joey Miskulin, but he was a superior showman. In this field, it isn't music that counts so much anyway. I'd say that 90 per cent of your success depends on personality.

As the years rolled by, my bands would keep changing. The boys would spend a few years on the road, then decide to pack it in. That was okay. I understood. I was just happy that I was always fortunate to find outstanding musicians.

It would take this whole book to list them all, but here are some of the accordionists who were with me: Dick Sodja, Frankie Kramer, Eddy Stampfl and Richie Vadnal, all of Cleveland; Mike Zitkovich and Herb Eberle, St. Louis; Mike Popovich, Denver; Jim Maupin, Milwaukee; Roger Bright, New Glaurs, Wisconsin; Don Kotzman, Stauton, Illinois, and Joe Sekardi, Nason, Illinois.

Sekardi was a happy-go-lucky guy who was with me for about five years after Cardone left. He was a bachelor and all he needed to keep happy was an accordion, a crowd and three meals a day. Popovich is the son of some Denver friends who always put us up at their home, Mr. and Mrs. John Popovich. He made a lot of western swings with us. Zitkovich was a bashful Croatian in his early 20s. He was a really polished player and I would exploit his shyness by telling girls in the audience that he was single. I'd invite them to come onstage and give him a kiss. They would do it and Mike would turn red and green.

I found a terrific bass player in Pete Rogan of Rochester, Pennsylvania. He was without a doubt the finest bass player I ever had. He was a serious musician, wrote music, and never drank. He was with me for about five years and helped me tremendously with arrangements. It was through Pete that I got hold of a fine piano player from Aliquippa, Pennsylvania, Emmett Morelli. He was cut from the same cloth as Rogan. Both are now living and playing in Las Vegas.

Ron Sluga was another exceptional side man. He was a good-looking young banjo player and singer from Cleveland who got as much fan mail as I did. He was a real sex symbol for the younger girls. When I had a weekly TV show at WGN in Chicago, they told me I could bring in only one man from my own band. It was a union rule. So the one I always chose was Sluga. That's how popular he was.

For about fifteen years we played about eleven months out of every year. We'd be gone from home for as long as four-and-a-half months at a crack, playing cities and hamlets from coast to coast. Every once in a while, we'd come home for a few days and renew auld acquaintance with our families.

I understood it was tough on my wife and kids, but they had to understand me too. I was either in the business or I wasn't. I couldn't do anything halfway. Either I had to forget about it and stay home, or I had to keep going. I chose to keep going because I wanted to see what life was like at the top of the mountain. I wanted to go all the way.

When I think back to those times I always remember the crowds. No matter where we played, whether it was Rock Springs, Wyoming; Trinidad, Colorado; or Youngstown, Ohio, we always had a full house.

We played almost every night. The ballrooms were all jumping. We'd perform before 1,000 people in Duluth, Minnesota, on a Sunday, and have to be in Regina, in Saskatchewan, Canada, on Monday. That's 800 miles. We'd finish one job and be driving to the next one at three in the morning.

We traveled in big black cars, Cadillac or Packard limousines that looked like hearses, and we'd tie the instruments on top of the car. Later we got a trailer and kept the instruments in the trailer. We used to say if we ever wrote a book it would be called "If the Trailer Could Talk."

We would sleep in the cars, but we'd try to get into a hotel every day, to clean up and do our laundry. We always used nylon shirts and underwear – drip and dry material – so we could wash them fast ourselves and not worry about ironing them. Many a time we had to skip a meal to make a playing date.

The longest trip we ever made was from San Francisco to a town outside Regina, about 1,400 miles. We drove all day and all night to get there and were only a half hour late.

We were less prompt when we went to Menomonie, Wisconsin. We made a mistake and drove to Menominee, Michigan, about 250 miles east, instead. When we got to the town in Michigan there was no ballroom. That was when we realized we were in the wrong town.

So I called the ballroom operator in Menomonie, Wisconsin, and told him what we'd done. He said, "Frank, you drive here as fast as you can. We'll wait for you no matter how late you are."

I told him we'd never make it, but he insisted he wanted us. He said he would have a substitute band there until we arrived, to hold the crowd. We piled into the Packard and I took the wheel. I had the guts. I was a fast driver, without a doubt. I didn't let anything get in my way when I was in a hurry. If I had to, I'd go 100 miles an hour.

We drove Route 29 full out all the way. Cardone, Griebel, Leslie and Paradiso were on pins and needles. We got there two hours late, but a tremendous crowd was there. We had a great time. I was glad we didn't disappoint them.

Another time we had to go from St. Louis to Duluth. I had business ahead, so I took a plane and let the boys drive up. I did that once in a while. When the boys left St. Louis at 2 a.m.

the weather was perfect, but the farther north they went the colder it got. They ran into a big snowstorm and didn't make it to the ballroom in Duluth until eleven that night, three hours late. When they came to the dance I was already playing with three other musicians I had picked up in Duluth.

With all the traveling, there had to be mixups. Once, Roger DiBenedict, one of my banjo men, went off with some friends in Traverse City, Michigan, after we'd played a job. Meanwhile, me and the other Yanks drove 150 miles south to our next job in Coloma, Michigan. We thought Roger's friends were going to drive him down. But they didn't. They dropped him off at the motel we were staying at in Traverse City. Roger thought we were still there. He was under the impression we were leaving in the morning. When he found out we were already gone, his friends had left. Roger had to hitch-hike 150 miles.

It was inevitable that we would pick up some speeding tickets. Usually we talked our way out of them, but if we couldn't we'd go to the local police station and pay up. Once I was embarrassed.

We were playing at the Stardust Motel in Vegas and I was lounging at the pool in the afternoon. A man walked up to me and said I owed him one of my record albums. I didn't know him from Adam.

"Don't you remember me?" he said. "I'm a state trooper from Pennsylvania. I stopped you once for speeding and you said if I let you go you'd mail me an album. I'm here to collect." He had me there. He got the album. I had forgotten all about it.

It wasn't always funny though. We rushed so much from place to place that we took some bad chances. I guess I was the biggest offender. I would pass on hills and go around curves at high speed. It's a wonder we weren't all killed several times.

Our closest call came in 1954 in Wisconsin. We were in a big hurry one night and it was raining. We couldn't see too well. We were crossing some railroad tracks and suddenly we saw a train. At first I tried to stop, but I saw it was too late. We all yelled and I stepped on it and swerved hard to the right, away from the train. We just beat it, but our trailer went off the runway and turned over on the tracks. All of our instruments were scattered around, but none were damaged. The train stopped and people got out to see if we were all right. They helped us pick up the trailer.

Tops Cardone was really shook. He made the sign of the cross. Then he blew up and started yelling at me. We almost had a fight. I couldn't blame him. It had scared the daylights out of all of us to see that train bearing down on us.

Tops said he was quitting the band right there and the other boys were almost in agreement. We finally came to a compromise. They insisted I do no more driving. I agreed. I never drove again until Cardone's last day with the band, in 1956. We were traveling from Olean, New York, to Cleveland. It was a sad day, with Tops leaving. I asked the boys if I could drive for old times sake, and they said okay. I drove all the way, never going over 50 miles an hour.

But I wasn't the only one who had problems with the car. Leslie once fell asleep driving and woke up just in time to miss hitting a semi head-on. We were all asleep. When Al woke up he was on the wrong side of the road.

Another time Leslie hit a deer in Wisconsin when he was going about 70. Cardone hit a couple of horses in Pennsylvania, killing one. The damage to the car was about $500 each time. I didn't get mad about it. We'd just keep going and when we got to a place where we could stop for a day we'd have the car repaired.

Paradiso was at the wheel once when a truck hit us, and we could have been killed another time when a swarm of Canadian Soldiers stuck to our windshield. We couldn't see a thing. We had to stop the car to clean them off. On still another trip, when DiBenedict was with me, our driver fell asleep on a job in Canada. I can't remember who he was, but it wasn't me. We were all asleep and then somebody yelled and we looked out and we were in the middle of a cornfield, with six-foot stalks all around us. We were 'way off the road and it was 40 degrees below zero. We had to go outside and push the car and trailer back on the road. But it was so cold we could only stay outside for a few minutes at a time. It took us a couple of hours to get back on the road.

In all those years we missed only one job because of an

accident. That was in 1958, when we were hit by a car in Rootstown, Ohio. We were on our way to play in Johnstown, Pennsylvania. Stampfl, DiBenedict, and Mike Dragas were with me. My Lincoln Continental was pretty badly banged up, but I thought we could still make the job. We got a crowbar and tried to pry the fender off the wheel, but we couldn't. It was impossible. We had to cancel.

During most of those days on the road, we took turns driving. Each man would be at the wheel for two hours, while the others sat and slept. A lot of the driving time was working time for me, though. I was always answering fan letters and doing band business in the back of the car.

I had bought myself a typewriter and taught myself to type. I'd sit in the back seat of the car with a typewriter on my lap and bang away, sometimes for as long as eight hours straight. I answered every fan letter I got, whether it was a good one or something silly. I want people to know that I appreciate them and I don't want them thinking I'm better than they are.

Sometimes people would tell me to get a secretary to handle all the correspondence, but I didn't want that. My business was so personal that people wouldn't accept that. They preferred my letters with all the typing mistakes, to cold, impersonal notes from a secretary that were perfectly typed.

I would type letters of thanks to people who had been hospitable to us in a town we just left, and I'd type letters to people we were going to be visiting in a few days. We'd mail the letters from each town we went through.

Once, when we were in Colorado, we had a little extra time and somebody wanted to take a scenic route. We wound up driving on a mountain cowpath. The road was so bad the car couldn't go more than about five miles an hour. DiBenedict said he needed some exercise and went outside and ran alongside the car. I didn't pay any attention because I was typing in the back seat.

Then the path got a little better and our driver started going a little faster. He forgot about Roger, who couldn't keep up. He was far behind. When I noticed Roger was out of sight I had the car stopped and we all went outside and sat down by a little creek for some fresh air. When Roger showed up I was sitting by the creek, typing. When I saw him I said, "Well, fantje, (boys) it's time to go."

Even today I answer every piece of mail I get. If I go on the road for more than a week, my mail is forwarded to me. I've always believed in the power of communications, and I always functioned as my own public relations man. I wrote letters to disc jockeys such as Kenny Bass in Cleveland and Eddie Blatnick in Chicago, telling them where we were playing and how we were doing. As often as possible, I'd go on the air with them. I still do that today, though not as much.

I always had a lot of news for the disc jockeys, and I kept a list of deejays all over the country. I must have had a hundred of them in my little black book, with all their telephone numbers and addresses. I would tell them about all the out-of-the-way places we played in.

In Bimidji, Minnesota, for example, we played in a 40-foot-by-70-foot room which was warmed by a coal stove. All the lumberjacks squeezed in. Once we played on an Indian reservation at Wolf's Point, Montana. Every year we would go to upper Michigan to play a dance for a hunting club. They always gave us hunting clothes to wear while we played, complete with checkered shirts, red caps and suspenders. The next day we would be the club's guests for hunting. I got a deer once.

One of our weirdest experiences came the first time we played in Leadville, Colorado, high up in the mountains. We always played sets of three waltzes, then three polkas. But we noticed that the people would quit dancing after the second song and go to the bar. We couldn't figure out why. Then we noticed that we were getting tired. We always did a lot of jumping and kicking and knee bends on the stage, but this night we were gasping for breath. Then it came to us. There was a lack of oxygen because we were so high in altitude, 11,000 feet above sea level.

People often ask me to name the biggest thrill of my career. I can honestly say that I had my greatest thrills playing for people who were glad to see us and appreciated our music. I didn't care where it was, in the Mocambo in Hollywood or the

Prom Ballroom in St. Paul, Minnesota.

Wherever we went, we had friends. I can't stress that enough. We weren't like other bands, strangers passing through town. When we came to a city, it was an event. Frequently, the local Good Time Charlies would mark the occasion with a celebration at our hotel.

I almost lost Griebel, my fine piano player, because of that. It was in Toledo, on Buddy's first night on the job. We played at a dance, then went back to our hotel. We had only a short trip the next day, so I invited a few Toledo pals back to the hotel for a party.

Griebel suddenly found himself in a room with eight jolly strangers, all of them drinking and smoking and having a good time. The night went on and on and Buddy wound up sleeping on the floor of his room, with the Toledo crowd sleeping on his bed and in all the chairs. Buddy was upset, but he got used to it.

That kind of scene was repeated in a lot of places. Eddie Habat likes to tell a story about a night in Detroit. A bunch of the guys had been whooping it up and they fell asleep in my room. In the morning a maid walked in and saw us all lying around without any clothes on, sleeping it off, naked as jaybirds.

The boys were embarrassed. They ran into the bathroom to cover themselves up. I couldn't understand why they were so embarrassed. I stood up and said, "What's the matter with you guys? Didn't any of you have mothers?" It broke everybody up.

Seriously, though, drinking was always something we had to be careful about, especially in our early days. We'd constantly be invited out by the people we entertained. They would treat us like kings and party with us until four in the morning.

When we were young, it might have been all right. But later it was a bust. You couldn't party all night if you had another job in another town the next day. You wouldn't be able to produce. Even if you were hung over the next day, the public didn't care. You had to look good. You had to smile, even if you were dying inside.

One thing I never could put up with was having my musicians go to the bar and drink overtime during a job. People don't go to a dance to watch musicians drink. In the old days, if the band stayed at the bar too long during intermission, I'd go back on the stage and start playing myself. I'd be singing and smiling and playing all alone, and they would come running out and join me, embarrassed.

I didn't do it to be mean. I felt we owed it to the crowd to play – not drink. If I told them to take a 20-minute break, I meant 20 minutes, not 25.

I guess I've softened up some. Today when the boys stay in the bar too long, I signal them to come back by playing a few chords.

I had learned the dangers of whiskey a long time before, back in the days when I was playing for Heinie Martin on WGAR radio. The staff threw a Christmas party and I drank scotch for the first time. I was only about 21. I got so sick I never touched it again. I had to play that night, too, at the Collinwood Slovenian Home.

I seldom drank any kind of booze after that. I preferred sparkling burgundy. But once I did drink a lot of whiskey and it caused me to miss a job for only the second time in my career. It wasn't really my fault.

I had an engagement at the Hollywood Supper Club in Chicago and in the afternoon I flew home to spend a day with my family in Cleveland. John Pichman, who owned a window company in Warrenville, Illinois, flew me back and forth in his private twin-engine plane. The band was already in Chicago.

But when we took off from Cleveland we ran into a terrific storm. There were four of us on the plane, plus several bottles of Seagram's Seven Crown. We were all scared to death. That little plane was pitching and tossing all over the sky.

The Seven Crown was our salvation. It calmed us down a little. But we couldn't land in Chicago. The airport was closed so we had to put down in South Bend, Indiana. By that time I was really loaded. I was never that smashed in my life.

We drove to Chicago and went to Joe Ziomek's house to clean up. Joe was one of my Chicago buddies. But when Joe

The band mingled with stars during its Hollywood fling in 1950 (left to right): Buddy Griebel, Yankovic, Bob Hope, Marilyn Maxwell, and Al Leslie.

Frank as Slovenian Man of the Year, Cleveland. From left: John Spiller, Yankovic, Jimmy Jerele, Congressman John Blatnik of Minnesota, and Frank Yankovic, Jr.

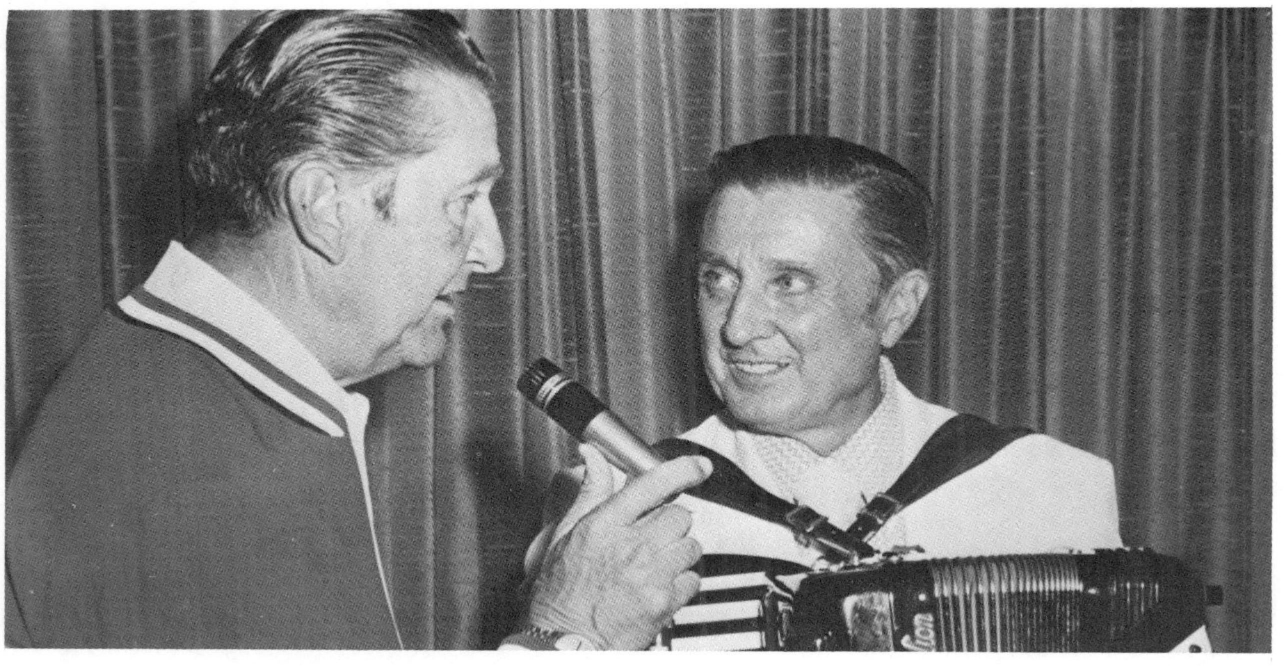

Lawrence Welk sharing the stage at Frank's steak house. Yankovic has appeared on Welk's television show several times.

Yankovic relaxing at a poolside party at his home. Others, from left: Frank Novak, Paul Wilcox, Kenny Bass, and Marty (Kukovich) King.

Walter Ostanek, Canada's Polka King (left), is a good friend of Yankovic's, and the two monarchs have performed together many times.

Frank Spilar, Yankovic's second cousin, was like a second father to his children.

The Marlin Sisters recorded "The Blue Skirt Waltz" with Yankovic in 1949, then dropped out of sight.

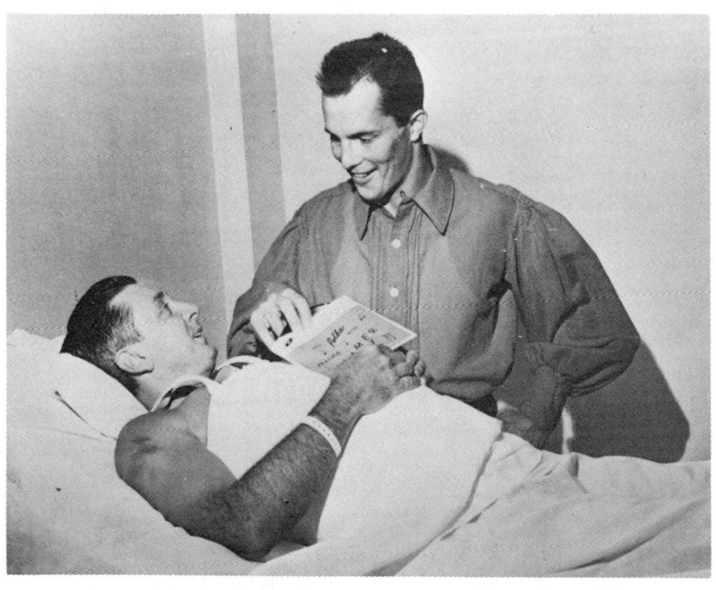

Accordionist Frankie Kramer was one of the many visitors to Yankovic's bedside in Cleveland's Huron Road Hospital following a serious auto accident.

saw me he put me right to bed. He didn't want me to go on the stage and look bad. So the band played without me. The owner of the club turned me in to the Musicians Union and I had to pay a fine of $500. I also lost the money I would have been paid if I had worked.

My musicians would become a problem from time to time, of course. It was hard to find men who could take the strains of living on the road. They would get homesick, or moody, especially in the daytime. I wouldn't know what to do for them. They would start mooning about their wives and children and they'd be writing letters to them all the time. At night, with all that in their heads, they would look awful on the stage.

Most of the boys would snap out of it, but a few didn't. One of the worst travelers I had was Paradiso. Carl was a great musician and one of the best singers I ever had, maybe the best. But he would have some awful days on the road. As a result, he just wouldn't respond to the audiences. Carl stuck it out with us for four-and-a-half years, though, and then was replaced by Eddie Teener. Teener was another bald man and I bought him a toupee too.

I sympathized with the fellows and tried to keep them as happy as possible. Whenever I could I booked jobs around Cleveland so their families could visit them. And I always made sure they were well paid.

I was paying the boys $145 a week when members of big bands were getting $75. As time went on, the Yanks were making $45 a night. DiBenedict recalls a day when he made $389 in one day. We had a recording session in the morning, then taped a TV show with Patti Page, Vic Damone and Ann Miller, and topped it off by working a job that night in Bridgeport, Connecticut.

All the boys felt happy with the kind of money they were making, especially since we were treated so well by friends on the road.

I know that Al Leslie, who was with me from 1949 to 1956, used to limit himself to $25 a week spending money. He would send home the rest and was able to buy himself a beautiful house. It was easy to save money for the side men. I paid for all the travel and motel bills. All they had to pay for was meals.

Leslie likes to tell about a week when we played in St. Louis. The people really enjoyed us there, and we were invited out for meals constantly. Leslie spent only $2.50 all week.

I would pay the boys every Monday, by the way, usually by check, occasionally in cash. I never missed once. I would take out the withholding tax for them too. I kept track of everything myself. And every Monday, without fail, I would send a $500 check home to my wife June.

If I saw the boys were getting a little depressed from the travel, I would try to take their minds off it with a little golf tournament for the championship of the band. We'd set up handicaps and I would buy trophies. Paradiso could shoot about 80, but Cardone was our best golfer. He was always in the 70s.

Once I took Tops with me to the Plantation Country Club in Ft. Lauderdale, Florida. We were guests of Leo Gocar, a friend from Detroit. Gocar and a partner wanted to play me and Tops for $50 each. Tops didn't want to risk that much, so I covered the bet. Tops shot 73. We each won $50.

Whenever we played in Ely, Minnesota, another of our favorite spots, I'd arrange to take the boys to a beautiful lodge that was nearby. It was operated for some business executives I'd come to know and we would take a 20-minute plane ride to get there. I'd pick up the tab for a few days of golf, hunting and fishing.

I knew the boys were sacrificing a lot for their families, so I tried to be as generous at all times as possible. I always gave them nice Christmas presents, for example. One Christmas I bought Cardone, Griebel, Leslie and Paradiso each a diamond ring. Another time I bought them a musical instrument of their choice. Griebel, the pianist, took a clarinet. Another Yule I had them pick out the finest material from a classy men's store and I had them fitted and bought them sport coats.

Any time a band member had a birthday I would take the whole band to the best restaurant in whatever town we were in. When we played in New York, I'd suggest to the boys that they bring in their wives. I'd fly them out and put them in the hotel. We would have dinner at a restaurant like "21" and I would make sure to have a corsage for each of the wives. I paid for everything. I prided myself on being a good host.

I really surprised Leslie one Christmas. I knew he wanted a trailer for his speedboat, so I drove all the way to Detroit from Cleveland and bought one from a friend of mine. I attached it to my car and drove it back to Cleveland and gave it to Leslie. He couldn't believe I'd done all that for him.

Another time, DiBenedict promised his daughters he would get them a collie dog. I arranged to get him one from some people I knew in Chicago. Roger called his daughters in Cleveland with the good news. They were thrilled, naturally.

But when we got to Chicago to pick up the collie, my friends had changed their minds. They said their children had begun crying at the thought of giving away their dog. So now Roger was stuck. We were going back to Cleveland the next day. What was he going to tell his children?

That night we played at John Korosa's Club Irene, and I got on the microphone and made an announcement. "Attention, everybody. We gotta have a dog," I said. "It's a matter of life and death. Does anybody here know where we can get a dog?"

A guy in the audience who owned a pet shop piped up and said he had one. He ran out of the lounge, went to his store and got a terrier puppy. We put it in a box and Roger took it home to his daughters.

Naturally, living close the way we did, we'd have our moments of temper. We were just like a family and sometimes we'd get on each other's nerves.

We were playing in Twin Falls, Idaho, and Leslie was having trouble with his amplifier one night. He couldn't seem to get it working right. At the end of the job I jumped on him and told him to hurry up and quit fooling with it. Al saw red and grabbed me by the lapels. But then he cooled off. I just smiled at him in a cocky way and walked off. I forgot it fast. It didn't mean anything.

Another time, years later, I had a piano player who was with me for about two months. One day, all of a sudden, he said he wanted to quit and go home. I got mad because he didn't give me any notice. It wasn't fair. It's not that easy to find good piano players. So we had a little fist fight and I knocked him down. The next day he apologized and stayed on for a while until I got a new man. That's the only fight I can remember having. Some of the boys had fights with each other. None of them were about anything important.

One of my nicest experiences came just before we made our first big trip to the West in 1950. We were playing at the Skyway Lounge in Cleveland and the old Collinwood neighborhood gang tossed a going-away party for us. Everybody chipped in and bought us a floral bouquet shaped like an accordion. Patsy Krall and Shorty Debenak, two boyhood friends, presented it to me on the stage.

People always ask me what it was like playing in Hollywood. They figure it was the high point of my career, and I guess in a lot of ways it was. After all, how many polka bands get the chance to play for the likes of Joseph Cotton, Rosalind Russell, Lana Turner, Ann Sheridan and Jane Wyman?

We made it to filmland with the help of Arthur Michaud, a big-time theatrical manager who had handled Tommy Dorsey, Henry Busse and other top bands. I never believed in managers or booking agents. I hated to give away a percentage of my money to a guy who did nothing for me that I couldn't do for myself.

But I hired Michaud and he was worth it. He knew the ropes in Hollywood, who to contact and who to put the bite on. Without him, we never would have cracked through. Lawrence Welk had a fellow like that too – Sam Lutz. Lawrence would be the first to tell you that a good manager is worth his weight in gold.

With Michaud's help we made a movie short for Universal Pictures, and we performed at the Lick Pier Ballroom in Santa Monica and the Aragon Ballroom in Los Angeles. We played the Aragon for months, and on Monday of each week we were booked into Hollywood's famed Mocambo night club, the movie stars' playground.

I was actually scared when we opened at the Mocambo. You have to remember that at that time Hollywood was the absolute center of the entertainment world. Some of the most famous people in the world lived there, and I knew there weren't going to be any polka people in the Mocambo. I didn't know how they would react to us. I decided we would do our regular thing and see how they liked it. I'm awfully proud to say that those movie stars really ate up our music.

Here's what the Los Angeles Herald Express said about our opening night at the Mocambo on June 18, 1950:

"The Hollywood stay-up-late crowd woke up seeing spots before their eyes after the dottiest night in the history of the Sunset Strip.

"That old time skip-and-jump, the polka, got the revival treatment at the Mocambo and all the people were invited to turn out in polka-dotted ties and dresses.

"Frank Yankovic, America's polka king, and his band rolled out the barrel and everybody had a lot of fun.

"To the strains of 'Hoop De Doo,' 'You Are My Sunshine,' and the 'Milwaukee Polka' people like Betty Hutton, Diana Lynn, Lou Nova, Ann Sheridan, Joi Lansing, Jane Wyman and Lorraine Cugat panted and puffed around the dance floor. Then they joined hands in a big circle like a bunch of farm-hands after a hard day of plowing the South 40."

We had them in the palms of our hands after the first number.

They were very publicity-conscious in Hollywood. For instance, me and the boys were brought to the Mocambo on opening night in a cart pulled down Sunset Boulevard by a donkey. When we got to the Mocambo, we were greeted by a squadron of newsmen and photographers. Roz Russell was there to say hello and get a little publicity.

I wasn't shy about doing my bit for publicity either. Almost every night I would drop in on an unknown young deejay and chat with him on his radio show. His name was Steve Allen and he later became one of the biggest men in TV.

On New Year's Eve, after we finished playing at the Aragon, we were invited to play a party at movie star Joseph Cotton's house. We were one of several bands there. A different band played every hour. The Cottons had a fantastic house, with a six-car garage, tennis courts and a swimming pool built into the side of a mountain.

Everybody got bombed at the party. They had champagne by the gallon. Cotton kept coming over to us, slapping us on the shoulders and saying, "You sure you got enough to drink?" Those movie stars were no different from anyone else. They liked a good time.

Tops danced with Gene Tierney and Paradiso danced with Jennifer Jones. Buddy Griebel and Mrs. Cotton played a duet on the twin grand pianos. Lana Turner, Reginald Gardiner, Oleg Cassini, Cecil B. DeMille and Gilbert Roland were there too. Paradiso had a long conversation with Roland. He was one of his favorite cowboy actors. We didn't get home until seven in the morning.

People ask me if I ever made love to a movie star. The answer is no. I wouldn't have had the guts even if the opportunity presented itself.

In 1951, we cut an album with Doris Day on Columbia. We wanted her to record our songs because we were trying to prove that a big star could sing our kind of music and make a hit. But Doris' manager, Marty Melcher, who later married her, insisted we do songs like "You Are My Sunshine," "The Comb and Paper Polka," and "The Pumpernickel Polka." The only good one was "You are My Sunshine."

Doris was real nice to us and she looked great. She wore blue jeans and a checkered shirt and had her hair pulled back in a ponytail. She and Melcher had an argument over one of the songs and she shouted at him, "My part is not written that way. We're wasting time."

Then she walked out, saying, "I'll see you tomorrow, Buddy." She had become friendly with Griebel. The next day we cut the songs without incident. Paradiso sang a duet with Doris and she autographed his banjo. The session didn't prove anything, except that we could always say we recorded with one of the biggest stars in movie history.

We performed from time to time with a lot of big stars, people like Arthur Godfrey, Jackie Gleason, Cesar Romero, and Lauritz Melchior. It seems to me the bigger they are, the nicer they are. They know what it means to please people and make a person feel at home. They always joked around with us and made us feel like we belonged. I offered once to teach Bob Hope to dance the polka, but he said he was still learning to do the Charleston. When we played at the Wagon Wheel in

Lake Tahoe, Liberace and Jerry Colonna would come in to see us every night. They were appearing across the street. We d always acknowledge them when they came in and the audience would give them a big hand.

In Milwaukee we played against the great Duke Ellington Band in one of those jazz versus polkas contests. We were in my territory, so we won. But later Duke said to me, "Frank, you've got the liveliest music I've ever heard. I wish I could turn people on like you can." It made me feel good.

We ran into another band which wasn't that nice. Like I said, the little guys are the meanest. We were playing at the Stockman's Hotel in Elko, Nevada, and were sharing the bill with an unknown jazz outfit. They frowned on us because we played polkas. They thought we were squares.

One night when they got off the stand we played the same number they had just finished with, and did it better. That really opened their eyes. When we got off the stage they asked us all kinds of questions about our music. They wanted to know why we didn't play jazz. DiBenedict told them, "We know where the money's at." We were making much more than the jazz band.

We met people on the way up too. For instance, we got to know comedian Don Rickles when he first started at the lounge in the Sahara Motel in Vegas. He watched our show many times. We also worked with singer Vicky Carr in Tahoe. She was plumpish then, and she dramatized her songs. A lot of times she would actually cry while she was singing. We were headliners at the Wagon Wheel in Tahoe when Wayne Newton and his brother supported us too. Wayne's brother was the star of the act. Wayne was the bashful one. Now of course he is a tremendous star. I don't know what happened to his brother. The Newton boys were so young then that their parents traveled with them.

We've crossed paths with Lawrence Welk many times, of course. In fact, he followed us into the Aragon in L.A. the first time we played there. I've been on his television show four times. He says I have a beat nobody can touch. Lawrence always said he wanted me to cut an album with him. Maybe some day we can still do it.

I once sang an old Slovene folk tune, "Ko Psi Zalajajo," on Welk's show. Eddie Kenik, a famed Slovene singer from Cleveland, was with me on that trip and he listened to me rehearse the song.

Kenik is a stickler for the Slovene language and he didn't like the way I was pronouncing the words. "That's awful," he said. "You can't go on singing the words like that. You better practice some more."

So we practiced for another half hour. But no matter how hard I tried, I couldn't say the words the way Kenik wanted me to. Finally I said, "The heck with it. Let's do it Yankovic style." It was a big hit anyway.

You wonder what Kenik was doing with me on the road? Well, it's not unusual for old buddies from Cleveland to come with me on trips. Fellows like Eddie Grosel, Joe Plesivec, or Al Jalen often come along when they can get away. I enjoy having them. Often, I pick up the whole tab. In the old days, I'd bring June and the kids out with me whenever I could too.

For several years in the late 1950s, Eddie Blatnick traveled with me. Eddie, a bachelor, was a good mixer and a good juicer. He also played a little accordion and had a weekly radio show in Chicago. He loved to come with us on the road. I always introduced him to people as my manager. It made him feel good.

Eddie was in California with me once when my piano player's mother died. The pianist had to leave to go home. We had about a dozen jobs left before the trip was over, so I said to Eddie: "You're my piano player."

"What do you mean?" he said. "I don't know how to play piano."

I told him all he would have to do is sit by the piano and pretend he was hitting the keys. We would put the solovox in front of his hands so people in the audience couldn't see them. "Just smile and sing our songs. You know them all anyway," I told him.

Eddie wasn't sure, but he gave it a try. Our first job with him was in the Rainbow Ballroom in Denver. Eddie got through the night beautifully. He really hammed it up. He continued as our piano man the rest of the way, except in Waukegan. "I refuse to do it here," he said. "Everybody knows me." But otherwise he was a great success. Nobody knew the difference.

A few months later, in fact, a woman came up to me when we played the Rainbow Ballroom again. She wanted to know what happened to Blatnick. "He was such a fine piano player," she said.

We had a great time with Eddie for several years. But then he had a couple of unlucky love affairs and he became ill. He's back in Chicago now, disabled. I haven't seen him in years. I don't want to see him. I want to remember him the way he was.

A lot of people say I'm popular because I always remember old friends. That could be true. I've paid my dues. When Ulrich Lube, for instance, was in the hospital for nine months I sent him a card from somewhere in the country every few weeks. Ulrich was an old friend from the days of the Wrong Club. When Ulrich's daughter got married, he asked me to play at the wedding. I made a 900-mile trip to do it, and all I charged was scale.

I always try to pay special attention to older people. It's tough to be old. I hope that when I get old, young people will pay me that consideration. I don't worry so much about youngsters. I figure they have youth, which is just about everything in this life anyway.

I did feel sorry for a young fellow once though. He was only about 14, and crippled. This was when we were playing in Tahoe in 1960. I'd see this boy at our motel and it seemed like his parents weren't paying any attention to him. I kind of took him under my wing and tried to show him some fun. He said he liked winter sports, so I even took him to the Winter Olympic Games that year in Squaw Valley, California.

It's always great to see somebody from the old home town when you're traveling around the country. Once I was playing in Fontana, California, and after the job I was invited to Joe Mlakar's bar. We had a jam session going when this young fellow from Cleveland, Zarko Valencic, came by and said hello. I'd just barely known Zarko in Cleveland, but we got to talking. I asked him if he'd like to come along to Vegas with us, where we were playing the next night.

He said he'd like to but that he didn't have the money. I said, "I didn't ask you if you had money. I asked you if you want to come to Vegas. The trip's on me." Money doesn't matter if I like *s*omebody.

Western Canada was one of our best territories for about seven years. We'd play in places like Regina, Edmonton, Saskatoon, Calgary, Medicine Hat, Moose Jaw, Bruno, Furr, Fulda, Lottbridge and Kenosee Lake. When we first went up there in 1952, there wasn't one paved road. It was all dirt and mud. Sometimes I think back and wonder how we ever got through all that. We'd be driving through mud or snow up to our axles.

We made it to Canada through a booker named Mickey Levine, who was running the Home Show in Duluth in '52. We were the show's headliners for a week and we packed 'em in like sardines. We sold our records by the thousands right across the bandstand. Mickey's father lived in Regina and he suggested we give Canada a try. The Canadians had a couple of very popular polka bands, Gaby Haas in Edmonton and Clem Gellowitz and his Happy Roaming Rangers in Regina. Mickey figured they would like us too. So he lined up a 14-day trip.

We started in Regina and drew 1,500 people on a Monday night at the Trianon Ballroom. That set the tone. The tour was a big hit all the way. There were a lot of Germans and Scandinavians up there and they really took to our style. The trip was such a smash that we had to play most of the same cities again on the way coming back.

We always enjoyed the Canadians. They were the greatest audiences. It seemed like they could let their hair down and have a better time than most Americans could.

We noticed that when we first played Canada that the hall would be empty when the dances started. We couldn't figure this out, since the parking lots were always filled with cars when we arrived. Then, about an hour after the dance began, the people would come in whooping and hollering.

We found out why. Booze wasn't permitted in the ballrooms at that time. So everybody would get tanked up in their cars. The mounties would ride around the cars in the parking lots with their flashlights, hoping to catch somebody drinking. Later, I understand, the law was repealed.

The Canadians were just great to us. Every time we played in Regina each fellow in the band would find a case of Carling's beer waiting for him at his hotel room. That came through the courtesy of a master brewer, John Bayer, whom we had met. The mayor of Regina was one of our biggest fans. Whenever we'd finish playing there, he'd invite us to his house for some more fun.

We don't get to Western Canada much anymore because the business has changed. It's just too far away now. There aren't enough jobs in between to make it pay off. Today you can't play seven days a week. The ballrooms are open only on weekends. Television killed them. So it just wouldn't pay for us to make such a long trip for only a few jobs.

It's a shame, because I know the Canadians would still welcome us with open arms. There's a disc jockey in Regina, Johnny Sandison, who wants to book us all the time. He's called The Morning Mayor. We finally got out to Regina for the first time in 17 years recently. It was a great trip. I'll tell you about it later in the book.

We made a big change in our travels in 1959, when I bought a 1937 bus in Red Lodge, Montana. It was an old sightseeing bus that had been used in Yellowstone Park. I paid $775 for it. It was a bucket of bolts, with hard rubber tires and mechanical brakes. I figured that once we had it fixed up it would give us more comfort and protection than we had traveling in cars.

We drove the bus from Red Lodge to our next job in Denver, but we found it couldn't go more than 40 miles an hour. A fellow named Wayne Motley, whom we met in Denver, had a custom body shop there. He took a liking to us and offered to fix up the bus—put in hydraulic brakes, a heater, air conditioning, power steering, and spruce up the engine. So we left the bus with him and drove on to our next engagement, at the Stockman's Hotel, in Elko, Nevada. We had a six-week job there and Motley was supposed to get the work done and deliver the bus to us in time for us to go to our next job.

Weeks passed and we didn't hear a word from Wayne. I

was beginning to get worried. I put the late Jock Justin, a Cleveland pal, on a plane to Denver to find out what was going on. I told him to stay there and check that bus each day, and to call me every day. On the day before we left Elko, Wayne drove in with the bus. The repairs he put in cost $3,000. Eventually, I put about $24,000 in improvements into it.

The bus was really a contraption, but it served its purpose. It had a big canvas top and we had "Frank Yankovic, Polka King," emblazoned on it. DiBenedict called it "The Ark." When we rolled into a town with it, everybody stopped and stared. It was good publicity.

We had beds put in across the width of the bus, so that the musicians could sleep stretched out. I kept the bus until 1967, when I donated it to St. Joseph High School in Cleveland.

Musicians came and went, but the travels continued. In the early 1960s, I met a 13-year-old boy who has become one of the finest all-around musicians and one of my best friends —Joey Miskulin.

Joey, who is of Croatian-Slovene descent, lived in Chicago with his grandmother and mother, who was divorced when he was four. The grandmother loved polkas and had a big collection of my records, along with those of Matt Hoyer, another Cleveland polka player who came along about twenty years before me.

Joey's mother and grandmother used to bring him to the places we played in Chicago, such as John Korosa's Club Irene. Joey would sit by the bandstand and stare up at me. I began to notice him. He was a good-looking boy and he reminded me a lot of myself in the days when I idolized Max Zelodec.

I got to talking with Joey's mother and grandmother, and learned that he had been taking accordion lessons since he was five. He could read music before he could read English. What's more, he had already played with a few bands in Chicago, like Roman Possedi, Charlie Ravens and Reddy Lee. In fact, he'd made a record with Possedi at age eleven.

The first time Joey played with the Yanks was at the Carousel Ballroom in Chicago, which was owned by L'il Wally. He was sitting there, staring at me as usual, and he asked me if he could play along. I suddenly announced to the crowd that we had a new young accordionist in the hall. I called Joey up and walked off the stage. He was scared to death, but his natural talent carried him through. I could see he was one in a million. He had a terrific ear.

Joey and I began to build a father-son relationship. He got so wrapped up in our music that he wanted to quit school and join us. That was impossible, but we did begin taking him with us, with his mother's permission, on summer vacations. The first job Joey worked with us was in Barberton, Ohio, in the summer of 1962, when he was thirteen. He was paid $50.

He stayed with us all that summer, as we traveled mostly around Minnesota, Canada and Chicago. I kept a protective arm around him, keeping him away from the rough stuff on the road. The other guys in the band would sleep in one hotel room and Joey and I would sleep in the other.

When the summer ended, Joey went back to school, even though he wanted to quit really bad and join me. On weekends he continued to play with us. I would fly him to whatever town we were in.

Sometimes Joey would talk me into letting him stay with me and he wouldn't go back to school for a while. His argument was that he was smart enough to skip school and still keep up with the class. He could miss a week, take a test, and still get an "A".

In the three years that Joey went to J. Sterling Morton High School in Berwyn, Illinois, he missed 234 days of school. Since there are only 180 school days a year, that means he missed about half his time there. But he still graduated, at the insistence of me and his mother. After he finished school, he was with me exclusively. He even lived with our family when we got back to Cleveland.

But in 1968, while we were playing at Harvey's Wagon Wheel in Tahoe, Joey said he was joining a Hawaiian group that was to tour the Orient. That news hit me. I was going through a series of crises in my personal life then, and this was another big blow. June had left me, and my mother was dying. I felt like I was losing all the people closest to me.

Joey hated to go. When he told me he was leaving, he

punched a hole in the wall of a motel room out of frustration. He said he had to join this group, that it was something he always wanted to do. He felt he had to prove himself in the musical big-time. So Joey toured the Far East for about eight months, then came back to me. He realized he could make more money and have more fun with my band.

Joey was with me for a few more years, but then he got married and his wife insisted he quit the music business. He took a job in a factory, and then sold insurance, but he was like a fish out of water.

After his divorce, Joey began working regularly again in Cleveland night spots, like Chef Ottino's. He's been playing the organ and singing at Ottino's nightly for two years. I told the people there that Joey was the best man they could possibly get. Joey also teaches accordion, piano and guitar. He doesn't want to go on the road regularly anymore, but he plays with me on TV in Cleveland and on a few Sunday jobs.

I know Joey consideres me his best friend. I was supposed to be his best man for his second marriage on January 10, 1977, but a snowstorm kept me from making the wedding on time. I was an hour late coming in from Chicago – so Roger Bright substituted for me. His new bride is Patty Hlebak, a beautiful girl who is a former Miss SNPJ.

I also met another young polka star in the early 1960s, accordionist Walter Ostanek, who is now called Canada's Polka King. Walter, believe it or not, was the president of my Canadian fan club when he was a teen-ager. Members of the fan club would pay dues of $2 a year and Ostanek would send them news clippings and pictures of all the Yanks.

I first met Walter when I'd fly to Buffalo in 1961 for a weekly television show I had on WKBW, Channel 7. I'd fly in every Monday to tape the show. I did 23 shows. Walter was there for 22 of them. He missed one because he was playing a job in the town where he lives, nearby St. Catherines, Ontario.

Walter would help me carry my equipment into the TV studio, set up the solovox, things like that. Sometimes he'd get me a bottle of sparkling burgundy from a bar across the street. After the taping, we'd go to Freddy Wneck's tavern in Cheektowaga, a Buffalo suburb, and have a jam session. The place would be jumping.

Walter told me that he had every record I ever made, except for the very early ones I did in the Heinie Martin era. The first record that he ever bought was my "Blue Skirt Waltz." He told me he stole the money from his mother's purse to buy it. Since the record cost only 89 cents, I don't think he'll go to jail. After Walter bought the record, he scratched the label so his mother would think it was an old one.

Ostanek, who is now 41, often plays with my band, especially on trips to Hawaii and New York. He was also with me for my stint on the Phil Donahue TV Show. And for nine months, Miskulin and I played on his TV show in Kitchener.

Ostanek justifiably deserves to be called Canada's Polka King. He is a fine showman and comes closer to matching my record for endurance than anybody. He logged 55,000 miles on the road in 1975, playing about 150 jobs.

But Walter wants to stay home more. He has a nice family and a music store in St. Catherines. More power to him. As I always told Miskulin, the musician's life is great for having a good time, but it's a mistake to make a full career out of it. It's too tough—unless your name is Yankovic.

Any worries I had in that regard nearly came to an end on July 29, 1963, when I was almost killed in a car crash in Cleveland. I was driving a Volkswagen, with my son, Robbie, then 8, and accordionist Don Kotzman as passengers. It was 4:30 in the morning and we were returning from a job in Kraut, Wisconsin. We had been driving all night. The bus was in Chicago for repairs.

At the intersection of Kipling and Ivanhoe avenues I tried to pass a police paddy wagon. Just then the wagon made a left turn and ran into my car. We were flipped over. I was thrown out of the car and landed on my back on the curb. My back was broken. I was the only one hurt.

I was taken to Huron Road Hospital and had to stay there from July until October, with a cast over my body from the neck to the waist. The doctor said there was a chance I might not be able to walk again.

Kotzman took over my band and fulfilled all my engagements.

The hospital nurses told me I set a record for cards received. I was getting 100 cards and phone calls every day. People sent me cheese and strawberry blintzes from Lindy's Restaurant in New York and I was getting steaks from Kansas City.

I had a secretary brought in and I dictated letters to her, answering all the people who were writing. I also discovered the clavietta, a musical instrument that I could practice on. It kept me from going stir crazy.

The clavietta is like an accordion, with 20 white keys and 14 black keys. The only difference is that you blow through it like a harmonica. It was perfect for me, since I couldn't move my body at all. The clavietta kept my fingers nimble and it enabled me to entertain visitors. We had a lot of champagne parties in my room.

I finally got out of the hospital after three months, just before my daughter Linda's wedding. I was still hurting. Even today, when the weather's bad, I feel the pain in the back.

CHAPTER X

BREAKUP

All this time my marriage to June continued to deteriorate. I could see almost from the start that our personalities weren't matched. She wasn't the type to be settled. Maybe she got married too young.

I wanted a real Slovenian-type wife, somebody who would give our kids the kind of secure childhood I had. I wanted a wife whose whole life was wrapped around the children—keeping the house clean, making good meals, and getting the kids to school on time.

June wasn't like that. She liked to stay up late watching television and then she'd sleep late in the morning.

I kept hoping June would change, but she never had a chance. Everybody spoiled her. She had a mother—God bless her—who was the type who would say, "Honey, if anything happens with you and Frank you can always come home to me."

June would take her up on that. Anytime there was any trouble between us she would go running to her mother. If she hadn't had some place to escape every time things got tough maybe things would have worked out better than they did.

My cousin, Frank Spilar, didn't help matters any either, although it wasn't his fault. Spilar, who was married and had kids of his own, was like a caretaker at our house. He'd come over in the morning and wake up the kids and make sure they went to school on time.

Spilar would dress the kids, make their breakfasts and wash their clothes and diapers. While he was doing the work for her, June thought everything was okay.

I didn't like it naturally. I'd try to straighten her out. That's why, when I came home, she would say to Spilar: "Hitler's home again." It particularly bugged me to see things strewn all over the house. I always was a neat person. I like things kept in place..

Our marriage problems went deeper than that, though. I kept hearing talk that she was doing things that a married woman shouldn't do. The talk bugged me from the start, even in the days before I went in the army. But I just let it go by. I wasn't the kind to look for problems. I figured what I didn't know wouldn't hurt me. Besides, she always denied everything.

I was willing to go along with her. I thought that if she was doing anything wrong she would change with time. I figured that our growing family would make her realize her responsibilities. As I said before, divorce was out of the question in those days. When I got married I thought it was for life.

When I went overseas June seldom wrote to me. Maybe once a month. She was working as a waitress at our bar and I heard stories that she was dancing up a storm and staying out late.

Eventually, June's letters stopped entirely. I didn't hear from her for about six months. I wrote to my parents and asked them what was going on.

They told me that June had taken our two children, Linda and Frank Jr., left our apartment on East 160th and moved in with her mother.

When I got home from the army on December 26, 1945, my parents and my lawyer, Anton Trivison, met me at the train. June wasn't there.

Nevertheless, I called June and went to my mother-in-law's house. June and I had a heart-to-heart talk. She said she hadn't written to me because she was fed up with the gossip and the way the bar was being run.

She said that she felt like a fifth wheel there, that my parents, sisters and Sam Slapic were taking over things and that she was neglected. She said she never wanted to work in the bar anyway.

We came to some kind of truce and she came back to our house. Things went on the same way. I'd play on the road and

I'd always hear the stories about her. I didn't know what to think. I didn't know if people were jealous of us and were making up stories about her just to start trouble or what.

I will say that June could be pretty clever. One time she came to a dance I was playing at out of town and wore a blonde wig as a disguise. I didn't even know she was there until later. I couldn't recognize her in the wig. That was a cute one. I almost have to laugh thinking about how foxy she was.

I don't want to blame June for everything, by no means. I knew it was rough for a housewife to live the type of life she had with me. It was a combination of her young age and loneliness that caused the problems.

If a certain type of guy came along at the wrong time I could see how she might go out with him – not for love, but for companionship.

Still, I didn't think that was a good excuse. Even though she was at home without me, she still had the children. I felt that the kids certainly should have given her all the love she needed.

A lot of married professional people were on the road as much as I was and besides, my life on the road wasn't all roses. It was tough for me too.

Further, I had stressed this whole thing before our marriage. I had warned June what our life might be like, that she would be alone a lot. But she insisted it wouldn't make any difference. She said she wanted to marry me and that she could handle it.

Whenever possible, I would try to make things easier for June. I'd take her on trips with us to Vegas or New York. I'd get home for short visits as often as possible. Once I sent her and a lady friend on a three-month vacation to Europe. I didn't believe in tying her down. If you can't trust somebody, it doesn't make sense to stay together anyway.

I've heard it said that June was roaming around in revenge against me. That's nonsense. I was no angel on the road but I never ran around the way people said I did. I never did anything that would bring disgrace to my wife or my children. In all my years of traveling nobody could come up to me and say I saw you do this or that. I held myself in respect.

Sure, I would do things on the job that were good for business. Girls would come up on the bandstand and I would kiss them or give them a hug. I always wanted to make people feel at home. What's wrong with giving someone a kiss in public on their birthday? It might not have looked right to some people, but there was always a show business reason for everything I did. When I kissed a girl it was all in fun, not from the heart.

The same was true in the hotels. The band would go into a fresh territory and when we came to town it was like a holiday. The girls wanted to be noticed. They wanted people to see them with Yankovic. They wanted to talk to me and kid around with me, so they could tell their friends they knew me. I'm not kidding myself that I had something extra. It was my position that impressed them.

When we would get to a hotel there would be all kinds of people waiting for us in the lobby – local big shots, young women, children, whole families.

We would have parties in our room, with all kinds of people there. They weren't private parties. The whole band would be there and a lot of guys and gals would come in. It was the same type of thing. They wanted to say they were with me.

There is no doubt in my mind that some of these same people who were so anxious to party with us on the road caused trouble for me at home. They would call June anonymously from all over the country and tell her that I did this or that. A girl who wanted to get next to you would look for ways to break up your marriage. They would call her anonymously and say, "June, I was out with your husband last night."

As circumstances developed in the late 1950s, I came to the conclusion I couldn't trust her anymore with money. When I was in my car accident in 1963, Spilar was the first one I called from the emergency room in the hospital. It was five in the morning and I was in a lot of pain. I whispered to Spilar to get my coat from the hook and look in the right inside pocket. There was $36,000 in checks there, the proceeds from a western swing I had just made. I told him to bank them and not tell June.

In the 1960s June became interested in a musician. This

fellow really became possessive of her. I had just bought a steak house and when I was on the road he acted as though he owned the place, ordering my kitchen help and bartenders around. Then he became ill and had to be rushed to the hospital. June was right there, getting a doctor for him and taking care of him.

That was when I really hit rock bottom. I didn't care about anything. All I could think of was that when I left the hospital with my broken back I went home alone in a taxi.

At that moment I made up my mind that June and I were finished. I decided that when things were right I'd get a divorce.

In 1968 June went to Detroit for a Bonnie Prudden health course that was supposed to last for ten days. She had been going there once a year for several years. She wanted to lose weight.

I was on a trip and I got home on a Monday morning. She was supposed to be home about the same time, but she didn't arrive. I thought nothing of it. I figured she was just late, and I got the kids off to school.

But she still wasn't home that night. Or the next night. Or the next. There was no word, nothing. The kids had no idea where she was either. So I called the Bonnie Prudden people in Detroit and they said yes, June had been there and, yes, she had signed out to go home. She had my Cadillac. I waited for eight or ten days and then I called my lawyer and he advised me to make a missing persons report. I went to the South Euclid police and did that. Still, there was no word from anywhere.

Just at that time I was having a swimming pool put into our back yard. I would come home at three or four in the morning and go to the pool to see how the work was progressing. I would notice that there were people watching me from behind trees. I found out later that they were police. They suspected that maybe I had killed June and buried her under the pool.

While all this was going on, my mother died at the age of 81. Mom's health had started to go downhill when she broke her hip. She was the kind who could never sit still. She always had to be doing something.

One day she started washing the aluminum siding on the back porch of her house on East 160th. She got a chair to stand on and when she stretched to reach she fell and broke her hip.

The doctors put a steel plate in her hip, but she wasn't healing fast. They said it was best to put her in a nursing home, so we put her in the best one we could find, the Western Reserve Nursing Home in Kirtland, Ohio, for $650 a month. It was nice, but my mother hated it because there weren't any other Slovenes there. She was lonesome.

So I tried to get her into the Slovene Home for the Aged on Neff Road in Cleveland, which was a SNPJ lodge organization at the time. But they wouldn't allow her in there because she was a bed patient. I pleaded with them to take her because she would be with her own people, but they refused me. I felt hurt, because I'd been so active in SNPJ. But I guess they had their rules.

Finally I got her into the Euclid Nursing Home, at 17322 Euclid Avenue, across the street from my steak house. I would take soup and wine to her every day when I was home. I had cut down a lot of the traveling by then. I didn't miss one day. The doctors said that it was okay to give her a little wine because it was only a matter of time. They said I should give her anything she wanted.

I was playing in Lake Tahoe when I got word that my mom passed away. I flew in for the wake and funeral. I thought for sure that if my wife was alive that she would be there.

June didn't show up, but I did learn she was alive. I got the news from one of my best friends, Al Rodway. I had been Al's best man when he got married years before.

When he came to the funeral home he said to me, "Frank, I feel like a heel, but I promised I would never say anything. I should have come to you sooner. I know that June is alive, but I can't tell you where she is. I swore I wouldn't. That's all I can say."

Wow! That news hit me like a sledgehammer. June had been missing for almost four months.

I hired a private detective agency and they went to work. They started out from the Bonnie Prudden School in Detroit and went from there. They knew my car and license plate number, of course. Little by little, the detectives found that June was staying with a man. It took them about three weeks to find her. It cost me about $1500.

When the detectives told me where she was, I got hold of my friend Joe Sonce, who had an auto agency in Detroit. He drove a tow truck to the house where June was staying and took my Cadillac to his garage. Then he called me and I drove out and picked it up. He never said a word to June. She never knew he was there.

It turned out June was living with a divorced man who had four children. He was an antique car buff and June had been introduced to him by Rodway. Rodway was a rich guy who was an antique car collector. June often went with Rodway and his wife to these car shows. It was there that she met this man that she was living with.

Naturally, I filed for divorce. We sent a notice to the address where she was staying in Detroit. She didn't contest the divorce. She didn't get a penny, after 28 years of marriage. It didn't cost me a red cent, except for attorney's fees. Later, she married the man. He is an artist and has his own studio.

After we found June, I had a meeting with the children. I told them where their mother was and I told them I knew I hadn't been much of a father, being on the road so much. I told them that if they wanted to live with their mother they were free to go with her. None of them wanted to go. They were all mad at her. Later on, they softened up. They often see her now. After all, she's still their mother.

June, in fact, came home once. It happened when I was on the road. She was visiting my son, Frankie, and his wife at their house. Frankie brought her to our home. My second wife, Pat, saw her. I thought it was a mistake on Frankie's part to bring her here.

I saw her about a year after the divorce. She and her husband came into my steak house. I didn't even recognize them as they walked in. I said, "Hi," like I did to all my customers. I was just walking into the office.

I was typing there and June opened the door and gave me a big hug and kiss. "How are you, Frank?" she said.

I nearly flipped. I told her to get out of there. I didn't want to have anything to do with her. They stayed in the steak house lounge for about an hour that night. Frankie and some of the other kids sat with them, but I didn't talk to them at all. I didn't want to give them any satisfaction.

The next time I saw June was at my daughter Andrea's wedding in Detroit. She came to me outside the church and said, "Aren't you at least going to say hello to me?"

I said, "Look, it's over. You mind your business and I'll mind mine. Let's not make a scene here." It was a beautiful wedding. She stayed with her crowd and I stayed with mine.

There has been no other contact. I told my kids, "When mom comes here I don't want to be embarrassed. Don't invite me over. I'm sorry, but that's how I feel. Nobody can change my mind. I had so much trouble that nobody even knows about."

CHAPTER XI

BOYS WILL BE BOYS

One thing people always ask me about: How did June and I find time to have so many children when I was on the road so much? When you combine that with the fact that June and I had a zillion marriage problems it's a legitimate question.

I suppose there are several answers. First, I never had that big love life on the road like people think I had. Second, even when things were going badly between us, for a long time I had a strong feeling for June. After all, I had married her. You don't marry somebody unless you think a lot of them.

Often, when I'd come home from a trip, it would be like having our honeymoon all over again. And June wouldn't try to avoid having children. Maybe we were thinking the same way. She was probably hoping that a bigger family would keep me at home more, and I was hoping that more kids might make June behave more like a mother. We were both disappointed.

I was on the road when seven of my eight children with June were born.

When Linda came along on November 16, 1941, I was playing at the Slovenian Home in Barberton, Ohio; Frank Jr. was born on October 7, 1942, while I was playing in Johnstown, Pennsylvania; we were playing the Village Barn in New York when Richard arrived on August 19, 1946; and I was changing planes in Chicago on October 17, 1948 when I got a phone call telling me that Andrea had just been born.

Jerry came on the scene February 14, 1951, while I was playing before a crowd of 6,000 at the Million Dollar Ballroom in Milwaukee; Mark was born October 17, 1952, while we were at the Crystal Palace in Coloma, Michigan; and Johnny arrived February 13, 1954, when I was playing in Monroe, Michigan.

I was in Cleveland when Robert was born June 5, 1955, but even then I wasn't quite there. I had flown in to attend Linda's graduation and I was at the ceremony when Robbie arrived.

I know the kids, especially the boys, resented me for being on the road so much. They felt I was never a real father, and I can't blame them. I couldn't expect them to understand that I was doing the best I could to make life comfortable for them.

One of my big troubles was that my time was so limited, even when I came off the road. I would be home for a day with so many things to do that I wouldn't be able to spend the time with them I should have. My desk would be full of mail. Even today it takes me a couple days to catch up on my correspondence and bookkeeping.

When a side man comes home, he's free, he's through. He can forget about his job and playing his instrument. I could never forget any part of my business.

Believe me, I tried to spend more time with the kids. I remember a couple of times when I'd dress up in a costume for Halloween and take the kids trick-or-treating. And I'd always try to be home for the Christmas holidays. We had some wonderful Christmases.

The kids never hurt for material things. They had the best clothes and I'd buy them new cars. All the boys, except for Frankie, went to Hawken School, a fancy private school on the outskirts of Cleveland. They even went to kindergarten there. The cost was about $1,700 a year for each one. It didn't mean a thing. It was just a waste of money. I couldn't see it, but June insisted on sending them there. I think she wanted them sent off to private schools so she would have more free time. Frankie, by the way, went to Grand River Academy in Austinburg, Ohio, and Benedictine High in Cleveland, a Catholic school.

If the boys resented me, I resented them too. They were being spoiled rotten and it bugged me. I was from the old school. My parents had given me certain chores to do and taught me how to keep my things in order. I wanted a house where everything was neat, in place, with everybody doing his job.

What got me the most was when I'd come home and they would be lying around watching television in the middle of the afternoon. The yard had to be taken care of, their clothes were thrown all over, their beds were unmade and there they were, goofing off.

I was like an army sergeant, strict. I thought that was what they needed. I would bawl them out and blow my stack. Sometimes I'd get on them for every little thing, hoping to wake them up.

If I'd known then what I know now, maybe I would have been different. Maybe when I came home, I should have talked to them quietly, played with them a little. Then, after a few hours, I should have gradually asked them why they didn't do this or that, or if anything was bothering them. Maybe we could have reached a better understanding that way.

There is no more of that old-fashioned discipline today. You can't get rough with kids. You have to talk to them. If you discipline them, they do less for you.

Me and the kids were never as close as we should have been. When I came home I would have liked to see them say something like, "Hi, dad. How was your trip? Are you tired? Is there anything we can do for you?" But there was nothing. No companionship. No feeling. They would say, "Hi" and continue whatever they were doing. Maybe I was asking too much.

I'd look at them lying around, griping, without a good word for me, and maybe I'd try to get back at them a little too. I'd praise some ten-year-old kid I might have seen playing the accordion in Milwaukee, or some teen-ager I'd seen playing the banjo in Sioux City, Iowa. Maybe I should have praised them instead. Maybe it all worked in their minds.

I don't really blame the kids, June or myself. It was just a bad deal all around. The boys are still young enough to make something of themselves. I hope they do. I'll help them all I can. They know that. But as of now, they haven't developed the way I hoped they would.

My oldest boy, Frankie, is a good kid, but he had this notion that he had to show me up. He was always competing against me, fighting me all the time. He wanted to show me he could go on his own and make it big.

I tried to teach him the restaurant business. First day there, he went behind the bar and was immediately going to show everybody how to run the bar, how to mix drinks.

Then he went into the frozen custard business, opened up a store. Same thing there. He thought he knew everything. Nobody could tell him a thing. Today he's a truck driver and he's making a good living, for which I'm grateful. He married a divorced girl who had three children. They've had two more children of their own and they seem to be getting along very well.

Mark has had his problems making it through adolescence like so many others in these hectic, fast-moving days—including a brief run-in with pals who had discovered marijuana. But all that is past now. Mark has the potential of becoming a fine man.

In 1969, when Mark was 17, I bought him and Jerry new Camaro Chevrolets. It was just after June had left me. I guess I was trying to make up for the tough time we had all gone through.

I told Mark and Jerry that I wasn't buying them cars to soft-soap them. I told them I needed their help. Some of the kids were still in school and I was depending on them to drive them to school and run errands. It didn't work out. Both Mark and Jerry railroaded their cars.

Mark's most publicized escapade came when he got into a fight with some police at the Cleveland Stadium during a Cleveland Browns football game. Here's the way The Plain Dealer of December 27, 1971, reported the story:

"Late in the game spectators and police had a minor melee. It started when George Gabuzda, 22, of 2077 Cornell Road, went on the playing field a few moments before the final gun. He was marched back to the box seat section by a policeman without incident—until a second policeman joined in.

"The vigor of the second policeman seemed to change the

mood of things. Gabuzda reportedly spit on an officer's shoe. The night sticks began to flail. Gabuzda was thrown between seat rows by three policemen, who battered him repeatedly.

"A friend of Gabuzda's, Mark Yankovic, 19, of 1544 South Belvoir Blvd., South Euclid, ran up the steps after joining in the initial encounter. He was caught by police and beaten.

"Gabuzda, Yankovic and two other men were charged with assault and battery on a policeman and with intoxication."

The newspaper also quoted a witness who said that the police acted with unnecessary brutality. Maybe that was true, but it was still another example of Mark getting into hot water when he shouldn't have. I had to admire the kid, though, for having the guts to help his pal when the police were beating him up.

After the incident, I went to bat for Mark and got him a top attorney, Sam Petrovich of Youngstown, and Mark was cleared.

Another time I was driving to Dunkirk, New York, with my second wife, Pat, and two friends, Ed and Nancy Grosel. I was playing a job in a Polish club there. But when we arrived I got a call saying that my kids had gotten into trouble back home and that the police were at my house.

I stayed to play the job, but Pat, Eddie and Nancy turned right around and headed home. They found the kids had gotten into my liquor in the swimming pool cabana. The kids got smashed and were yelling and running up and down the street. They were even selling my burgundy to the neighbors.

Mark got pretty sassy and Grosel slapped him across the mouth. Mark just looked at him and said, "My father never did that." Maybe he needed more of that. My punishment was almost never physical.

I don't see much of Mark these days. He is living in Kent, Ohio, and has taken some courses at Kent State University. He's also worked as a bus driver there. He comes to see me when he needs help or advice. I still have hopes that Mark will pull himself together someday. Nobody would be happier than me if he did.

Mark, Frankie, and Johnny all took accordion lessons, by the way. But they didn't keep at it. They had too many other things to do. Maybe they would have practiced more if I had been home to encourage them.

Johnny was also picked up a couple of times for marijuana possession, but other than that he hasn't been in trouble with the law. I don't even know if you can call marijuana possession being in trouble. A lot of people say it is no more harmful than beer, and that it should be legalized.

A couple of years ago, Johnny and Jerry asked me for $4,000 to start a landscaping business in Orlando. After a short time, they sold out and Johnny came back to Cleveland, to work as a mechanic.

I didn't even know where he was living when all of a sudden he came over and said, "Dad, I'm getting married." He didn't have a penny to his name but he wanted to get married. I had never even met the girl. I threw a big wedding for him on November 3, 1975 because he wanted one. But I'd rather have given him the $3,000 it cost. He could have made some use of it.

Jerry has had a lot of tough luck. He's lucky that he's alive. When he was 18 months old, on September 26, 1952, an explosion from a gas leak blew up his bedroom while he was asleep. He had burns all over his face, legs and arms. The shock from the explosion also gave him a double hernia.

When the gas exploded, Linda and Andrea were playing house on a porch downstairs. June, who was eight months pregnant, was on a couch. The blast broke the glass in the windows and threw the clothes in Jerry's room into the neighbors' yard.

Linda saved Jerry's life. She was only eleven at the time but she ran upstairs and got him. His clothes were smoking. Linda wrapped Jerry in a blanket and ran out on the street. A truck driver stopped and rushed them to Huron Road Hospital.

I was playing in Monroe, Wisconsin, at the time and I flew back right away. When I saw how badly Jerry was burned, I thought there was no hope for him. I'm glad I was wrong.

Jerry was in and out of hospitals for a long time. He had eleven skin graft operations. We hired the best doctor for skin grafts, a Dr. Ord Blackledge. He did a terrific job. Jerry looks almost perfect today. It's a miracle, really.

The East Ohio Gas Co. gave Jerry $22,000 because of the accident. We had sued for $300,000 but we settled after eight years because we were afraid we wouldn't get anything if we fought it out in court. I held the money in trust for Jerry until he was 21. He got $14,759.51. The lawyers got the rest.

Jerry got another bad break when he was 12. It was the day after Linda's wedding. He was playing football and the ball hit him in the eye. When we took him to a doctor, eye cancer was detected. They removed the eye immediately.

Then we had to rush Jerry to Presbyterian Eye Hospital in New York, one of the biggest eye hospitals in the world. He was given cobalt treatments to make sure the cancer wouldn't spread. Jerry also got an artificial eye at that time. They weren't making eye transplants yet.

The doctors said that Jerry was lucky that the football hit him in the eye. They said that otherwise the cancer would have gone undetected and that Jerry might have died.

Richard is the most financially successful of my sons, but it wasn't easy for him either. He had some mental problems for a while and I had to take him to a psychiatrist. We went to see the psychiatrist together. He talked to Richard first and then he talked to me. As time went on, Richard straightened out.

Richard left home at 17 and went to Chicago, where he lived for a year with my close friends, Carl and Ann Birsa. I paid his way through a hairdressers' school and it wasn't long before he got a good job.

Now he is one of the most successful hairdressers in Chicago. He works for the biggest and classiest salon there and he's making money hand over fist. He wants to open his own shop. He travels all over and lives with a friend in a $600-a-month penthouse apartment.

I'm proud of the kid. In fact, he's the godfather of my daughter, Teresa.

Next comes Robbie, who is living at home with Pat and me. He's a good kid, and he's working as a plumbing inspector. He plays the guitar pretty good and I suggested he take up the banjo too. I could get him jobs with me.

But Robbie doesn't want to do it. I think it's because he

hasn't been raised in an ethnic neighborhood. He doesn't want his friends in the sticks to call him a cornball. But Robbie surprised all of us at Johnny's wedding. He went up on the stage and played his guitar and sang and knocked all of us for a loop. He has the makings of a real good entertainer. When Joe White, one of my banjo players, heard him, he offered to give him free lessons.

Robbie has had his share of tragedy too. One of his closest friends was killed in a crash while Robbie was driving my jeep.

The accident happened on March 21, 1972. Robbie and seven other kids took the jeep, a Ford Bronco, without my permission. It was up on blocks in the garage. They took the cab off and spent the afternoon riding around. They were heading home when the jeep rolled over on a steep hill in Gates Mills.

Five kids, including Robbie, and Claude Tanner, 17, of South Euclid, were injured. Claude died four days later in Hillcrest Hospital.

We talked to all the parents involved and they all agreed that the accident couldn't be blamed on any one kid. They said they were all at fault and that they had no business going out there.

Bill Tanner, the father of the boy who died, said, "Frank, don't feel bad. My kid's just as responsible as yours." Tanner, by the way, is the executive news editor of the Cleveland Press.

Late in 1975, however, almost four years later, one family changed its mind. Robbie, my wife and I were sued for $204,-000. The suit is still pending.

For a long time after the accident, Robbie went through hell. He and the boy who was killed were very close. Robbie would leap out of bed, screaming, in the middle of the night. I had to take him to a psychiatrist to get him straightened out. Mr. Tanner was very good to Robbie. He encouraged him to come over and talk to him anytime he felt like it.

I got along with my daughters very well. Linda, the oldest, was more of a mother to the other kids than June. Like Spilar, she would get them off to school while June slept. Linda was a very quiet, conservative girl. She acted a lot older than her age.

Linda liked drama and singing, took it seriously. In fact, she sang with me a few times on Cleveland TV. Later she attended Alverno College in Milwaukee and graduated from the University of Detroit.

Linda married Henry Konrad, an electrician, in 1963 and had one of the most beautiful wedding receptions I've ever seen. When Linda said she was getting married I offered her a choice of a $10,000 check for a wedding present or a big wedding. She wanted the wedding, so I went all out. We invited 1,000 people to the reception at the LaVera Supper Club, outside Cleveland. Henry's dad was a grand knight with the Knights of Columbus.

Ten years later I treated Linda and Henry to a free trip to Hawaii on one of my polka tours. It was just a little present for them, in appreciation for being such a great couple. During the trip Linda and Henry fell in love with Hawaii. When they got back to the mainland, they began talking about moving there permanently with their five children.

Henry flew to Hawaii alone to see if he could line up a job. He got one and in 1973 the whole family moved to the Island of Maui.

As far as I was concerned it was a great development. Henry and Linda seemed to be the ideal couple. There was nobody more devoted. They spent all their time with their children. Whenever I was in Maui I'd stay with them, taking the kids on picnics and to the ocean.

Now comes the big surprise. In May 1975 I got a call from Linda. She said, "Dad, I've got a big surprise for you. Henry and I got a divorce." That flipped me. Twelve years of a fine marriage gone out the window.

I still can't believe it. Anybody who knew Linda and Henry feels the same way. Without a doubt this is the biggest surprise of my life.

Andrea, my second daughter, also dabbled in show business as a singer for a while. Most people remember her best for her singing during the first big testimonial ever held for me, in Belle Vernon, Pennsylvania, just outside Pittsburgh.

That was on October 6, 1968. Andrea sang all my big numbers while Sam Pugliano and Jake Derlink played. It was a surprise. I had no idea Andrea was going to sing. It was an emotional day, with people singing along. The hall was packed. June had just left me and this, combined with the music and all the accolades tossed my way, got to Andrea. She broke down in the middle of a song and cried. I have a tape of the whole affair.

Andrea left home as soon as she graduated from high school. She went to a business school in Chicago. In 1971, she married a fellow from Detroit, Michael McKinnie. He is a college graduate and has a good job with Ford. They live in Ypsilanti and are very happy. When I'm in the vicinity I drop in on them and stay overnight.

I always did have a good rapport with my daughters and now it looks like the boys are starting to come around too. As they get older, they understand me better. Now they can see how hard it is to make a living in this tough old world.

CHAPTER XII

FAMILY'S REPLY

EDITOR'S NOTE: *In this chapter we depart from our format of having Frank Yankovic tell the story. Frank thought that we should also interview his first wife, June, and his children. He suggested that we would have a good opportunity to do so at his son John's wedding at Diamond Jim's Restaurant in Cleveland on November* 3, 1975. *We attended and talked to June, Mark and Jerry. The other interviews took place at other places and other times.*

* * *

June came to the wedding without her second husband. She sat with her son, Frank, Jr., and his wife, Janet, and danced frequently with her children and old friends. She was charming and articulate and a little plump. The Yankovic children who were there looked like graduates of the All-American class, handsome, open-looking youths who seemed to know how to have a good time.

It was a bittersweet scene, with June and the children recalling life with Yankovic, while the King himself, accompanied by Miskulin, played the polkas and waltzes that had made him famous. The first song Yankovic played that night was "Bye-Bye, My Baby," the number he had sung to June the night before he went into the army nearly 33 years before. However, when he played the song June hadn't yet arrived. When she did come, Yankovic ignored her completely.

During the bridal dance the King came down on the floor and danced with the bride's mother. June danced with the bride's father, who suggested that June and Frank also dance with each other. June was willing, but Yankovic immediately got off the floor, frowning, and returned to the bandstand.

June came back to her table and said, "You see how he is? I'm hurt. I'd like to be friendly with him but he won't talk to me. I've walked up to him, like at Andrea's wedding, but it's no use. I'd try to talk to him tonight, but I don't want to make a spectacle of myself in front of the whole family. I have pride too. I don't understand why he is this way. Why make life harder? He has a new family now, so why not forget it?

"When I heard he got married again I sent him a card of congratulations, and I tried to call him on the telephone. But his wife said he wouldn't talk to me. In a way I feel sorry for her because she's going through the same thing now that I went through. I don't think Frank realizes he's still doing the same thing.

"Frank's a good person, too good. But our ideas were different. If he hadn't gone on the road so much, we'd still be together. I love my present husband but I love Frank too. You can love two people, the one you are married to and the one who was your husband for 28 years.

"After all, Frank is the father of my children. When I left him I didn't take a penny because I loved him. I couldn't take him for money. You can't completely forget what happened, but I couldn't live with him. He is the type of person you can't reach.

"Sometimes he'd be gone from home as long as six months. I had babies he didn't see until they were a month old. I would beg him to stay home, especially in the late 1950s, when the boys were growing up. But he wouldn't listen. He said he couldn't afford to quit yet.

"Every year he would promise that it would be his last year, but it never happened. Frank will die on the stage.

"He's done a tremendous job for his nationality and he's made people happy all over the country. But sometimes when you make other people happy you hurt those who are closest to you. Big stars are usually that way. It's something in their makeup. They don't mean to hurt you, but they do.

"Frank's family always came second. His friends came first. Sometimes you can get awfully tired of waiting.

"Frank was always determined to be a star and the ironic thing is that I encouraged him. It all started before we were married, when we were still going together. We went to the State Theater downtown to see the Glenn Miller Band, which was very big then. As the band played and got a big reception from the crowd, Frank said he wished he could do something like that. I told him he could do it if he really wanted.

"Then, in 1946, Columbia offered him the recording contract and asked him to travel. He asked me if he should go on the road. I said, 'Go, if it will make you happy.' I didn't want to hold him back. Maybe I should have, like a lot of other women do. But I never expected him to get in so deep, to the point where I hardly ever saw him.

"Frank sent me plenty of money, but I wasn't used to a lot of money. I didn't need it. It's not the most important thing. Having someone there when you need him is more important. Children can do only so much for you. They can't give you the emotional security you need, and which a man can give you. I would do anything and everything to get my mind off my loneliness. I took courses at John Carroll University and I worked with retarded children.

"Everything kind of worked against us – the separations, the war, the bar. Soon after we were married, I realized I was married to a bar owner, not a husband. That was bad too, because I never wanted to work in a bar and Frank expected me to.

"Then I started hearing things, that he had a girl friend at the bar and others when he went on the road. Don't believe it when he says I lost interest in him by the time he went into the army. No way.

"Eventually both of us became vindictive. We'd argue like crazy. When someone hurts me, I try to get back. I'd make him jealous, or ignore him. I wasn't an angel, but I was hurt. A lot of things that were said about me weren't true, but I let him think they were. I liked to dance and a lot of people liked to dance with me. I had to try something. Unfortunately, it didn't work.

"There were a lot of other little things that hurt our marriage. My mother was very domineering, for one thing. She and Frank never got along. Their personalities clashed.

"Frank's father was a generous, warm guy. A great guy. But

his mother was different. Foreign women are that way. She would give you anything, but it was hard for her to show affection. Frank was the same way. He was generous, but he couldn't show you how he felt. There's a big difference.

"The final straw for me came on our 25th wedding anniversary. I was working as a hostess at our steak house, and Frank was on the road. I hadn't heard from him, but somehow I was sure he'd show up for our anniversary. I thought he wouldn't book a job that day or, if he did, he would cancel the engagement. I had gone through so much for him.

"But I spent my 25th anniversary alone in the steak house. A bartender gave me my gift from him. That's what did it. That was when I got very cold and made up my mind that I would leave him when the time was right.

"I had tried to leave him before but he always talked me into coming back. I knew he'd never let me go. That's why, when I finally left, I kept my whereabouts a secret. I didn't want him to talk me into coming back again. There was nothing left.

"The only reason I didn't come back for his mother's funeral was that I didn't want to make a scene.

"I went back to our house on South Belvoir once. That was in 1973, when Linda moved to Hawaii. Frank wasn't home, but he called on the phone just when I walked in. I picked up the phone by the swimming pool, but he wouldn't talk to me.

"I have a very good relationship with my children, by the way. All my kids visit me two or three times a year. When I come to Cleveland I stay at my son Frank's house. He and Janet have a lovely family.

"Frank's absences were as hard on the children as they were on me. It's difficult for a woman to control a son, let alone six of them, without a father's help. I got a lot of help from Frank Spilar though. He practically raised the boys. His wife helped me clean when I was pregnant.

"Frank never understood his children. He either spoiled them rotten or punished them, but he never punished them in the good old-fashioned vay. He'd give them cars and then take them away.

"He should have sat down and talked to them. They'd give

anything to talk to him. But he always had his mind on something else. They still need him today. Mark needs him the most.

"I sent all the boys to very good schools because I knew they would get a man's supervision. They needed that. They needed more than just being told to get out of the house when they did something wrong."

She is asked to comment on Richard, her hairdresser son. "He had problems because Frank was away so much," she said. "Too much mama, not enough papa. Some children are more sensitive than others.

"I'm married now to an illustrator who has his own studio. He's a natural artist, in the same way that Frank was a natural musician. He went to art school for a year and a half and they told him there was nothing more they could teach him. He knew as much as the teachers.

"My new husband was born with club feet and wore casts until he was eight years old. He needed two operations before he could walk. He was married once before. He and his wife had four daughters before she left him.

"I'm very happy now. I have a wonderful husband. He understands me and he's very good-looking. He's known only two women – his first wife and me. We live in a beautiful house in Michigan and we have a big interest in antique cars. We have six of them."

June is asked what she would do differently if she could go back 35 years and marry Yankovic again. "I would never let him travel," she said. "I don't think he's happy. He's a very deep person. It's hard to explain. I want him to be happy."

* * *

Frank Jr. is a tall, gregarious fellow. He doesn't push himself forward, but once he is approached he talks freely. He is well-dressed and wears his hair styled in the modern fashion. He seems to identify strongly with his father.

"I have no resentment toward my dad for his way of life," he said. "He told me many times that he wished he hadn't gotten into it, but that it was all he knew.

"It's a funny thing, but I'm in the same predicament now as he was. I'm hardly ever home. I'm a truckdriver, hauling steel between Milwaukee and the East Coast. I'm on the road about five days a week. I turn down weekend overtime just so I can be home at least two days a week with my five kids.

"It was rough when I was a boy, but Frank Spilar pulled me through. He was like a second father to me. He'd take me to ball games and things like that. Then all of a sudden dad would come home and I'd have to switch to having a new father.

"Dad would come home from playing, traveling 500 miles each day, sleeping in his car, and as soon as he'd get home somebody would tell him about something that had gone wrong. He wouldn't even have time to sit down before somebody was telling him that one of us had broken a window or had a fender bender or something like that. He would explode.

"That's why I tell my wife now not to tell me about any problems when I first get home from the road. Let me have some coffee, let me unwind. Then tell me. I understand dad a lot better now.

"Dad was generous, but tough. He'd get mad at us if we didn't do things right away. He'd tell me to cut the grass, for instance, or take the mail to the post office. I would mean to do it, but then I would get sidetracked. I would pull a kid stunt, like phoning a girl or getting into a baseball game.

"Dad would see I hadn't done my little chore, so he'd go out and do it himself. I guess he was trying to make me feel ashamed. Then he'd send me to bed for punishment.

"Dad was never afraid of work. I never saw anybody with more energy. And he was a handy guy. If he saw a pipe needed fixing, he'd get right down in the grease and do it. I've seen him take his suit off in his restaurant and do some repair work like a laborer. He had the old way of thinking. He'd rather do it himself than pay somebody else. You have to give him credit.

"There was always something between dad and me. It goes back to the old European tradition that a man shouldn't show his feelings. I wanted more from him in that way. Instead, he'd give me things.

"When I graduated from Benedictine High I wanted him to be there. He tried to make it, but he couldn't. He was working in Vegas. So he gave me an F-85 Oldsmobile for a present.

"That was the European heritage. Parents never really showed love. I'm trying to reverse that with my kids. I try to show them I care about them. We hold family council meetings.

"Dad's so-called friends made a lot of trouble in our family. He would go on the road and tell his buddies to keep an eye on us. They were brown-nosers, so they told him more than was necessary just to get on his good side. They wanted him to know they were keeping close tabs on us.

"When dad was gone, I was in charge, being the oldest. One time the boys brought some girls over to the house. Nothing happened. Just some necking. No trouble. But somebody in the house stole something small, like a tape recorder or a radio. I can't remember what it was. Dad's friends told him about it right away and he got mad.

"Another time my brothers had a skinny dipping party in our pool. It was about two in the morning. There were no girls there. But the friends made it sound like it was a real wild party and dad got mad again.

"This sort of thing hurt my brothers the most. The friends would tell dad we were no good and he'd punish us. Then we'd badmouth him for believing the so-called friends. This wasn't right on our part, but there were strong feelings involved. My brothers wanted to love him, but they would say they didn't give a damn anymore.

"Sometimes I traveled with dad. He had friends on the road that were fantastic — the Birsas in Chicago, the Reberniseks in Wisconsin, the Spillers in St. Louis, people like that. I'd stay with them for two or three weeks. These people were real friends and I have great memories about those times. They were down to earth people, very good to me.

"Sure, I saw dad kiss girls sometimes when I was real young. We didn't understand that maybe he was only being sociable, and doing it to promote business. At that age we would tell mom.

"But I can honestly say I never saw either my mother or my father playing around on each other. Still, when you're hurt, you might bring up something like that in an argument.

"I had the burden of living up to dad. That can be tough,

especially when you're looking for a job and everybody is saying, 'What do you need money for? You're Yankovic's son.'

"School was tough for a while too because of my name. Then I became just one of the guys. I was on the track team. Even today when I drive into a town like Pittsburgh everybody knows me just because of my name.

"Mark comes to see me every time he has a problem. He gets pretty hairy. I calm him down. I don't want him to hurt what dad has gained.

"Basically, Mark wants dad to put his arm around him, instead of giving him something. He's being helped by a psychologist. He's got a head on his shoulders. I have a good bunch of brothers. I'm like their third father."

* * *

Mark Yankovic has the smooth, clear face of a handsome choir boy. A friendly, curious smile plays around the edges of his mouth. To look at him, you would never guess he's ever been in trouble.

"I live with a girl who's a senior in nursing at Kent State University," he said. "We've been together about two years. We may be getting married some day. She doesn't want to let me go and I'm starting to feel the same way about her.

"I'm working as a bus driver in Kent. I also have 69 hours to my credit as a pre-med student at Kent State University. I couldn't go to college this quarter because I had a car accident.

"I see my dad whenever I can and he helps me whenever he can. Lately we get along pretty well. But I'm lucky if I can find him. He's always on the move. He'll never stop for anything. He has to please the people. That's his profession.

"I got everything when I was a kid, too much. When I was 16 he bought me a new Camaro. I'd travel with him on the road too, and we'd have good times. But then we'd be separated. I'd have to go back to school.

"It messes up your mind a little after you've been on the road with him, having fun, and then he comes home and disciplines you. Then he leaves again the next day. You don't know where you are.

"I was with my mother all the time. Any gripes about him

came from her. I took her word for everything. She loved him a lot, but then they separated. Both are happy now, but they probably still have a feeling for each other.

"I'm getting to the point where I understand dad better. I see where he's coming from now. A lot of it was my fault. I never gave him a chance. I like him a lot. He tries. I used to pass judgment on him when he would take my car away for a week. I thought he was picking on me. That's how the trouble started.

"About the fight at the Stadium, me and my friends decided to get drunk. Near the end of the game we went out on the field to scream for a touchdown, to get things moving.

"The police escorted us off. But they got rough with my friend and he spit at one of them. There were eight of them and two of us. They were roughing up my friend and I tried to stop them. I took a club away from one policeman. If I wanted to, I could have broken his neck. But I could never do that to anybody. I never touched them.

"I was standing there innocently when it started. It seems like every time I turn around I find difficulty. I'm in the wrong place at the wrong time. I don't understand it. I think I'm a nice guy."

* * *

Linda lives on the island of Maui, in Hawaii, with her five children. She recently went through an amicable divorce from her husband of 13 years. As a full-time civil service employee, she is the director of the only children's theater in Hawaii.

"I don't think I had a bad childhood," she said. "There were some difficult times, but every family has good moments and bad ones.

"Dad was successful as a musician and as a personality and we all shared in that. We traveled, met interesting people and had a nice home.

"One of the disadvantages was that we couldn't always be ourselves. People were always aware of us as being Frank Yankovic's children, so we were probably more on edge and self-conscious. We weren't free to do things and just be anonymous. Maybe that's why I was a quiet girl.

"We had some wonderful Christmases. Every Christmas Eve, about one in the morning, Santa would give us our gifts. I would get the first present, because I was the oldest, and then we'd go upstairs and get the younger children, one by one, according to age.

"The kids would come down the stairs, rubbing the sleep from their eyes, and dad would be taking movies of them as they came down the stairs. The front room would look like a movie set filled with lights and cameras.

"We always had a lot of friends over and that was difficult. Sometimes we'd want to just be alone, but dad never seemed too happy with that. Pat says he hasn't changed. They still never have a moment to themselves. Pat's been very good for dad, and my mom is happier too.

"I like Pat very much. I find it very easy to talk to her, almost easier than to talk to dad. My children care for my mom, dad and Pat. My kids think it's just great that I have two little sisters, Teresa and Tricia, who are younger than they are. And I get a kick out of telling people that I have a sister who is younger than my youngest daughter.

"I love Maui and so do the children. I hope it doesn't offend anyone, but I don't care if I never go back to Ohio. I love the life style here and there are so many other places in the world I'd like to see. I guess I got the traveling bug from dad. If I could afford it, I'd travel all over the world.

"I'm also like dad in that I can't sit still. If he wasn't busy he'd fall apart. Dad says he wouldn't want to live in Hawaii because it's too quiet for him."

° ° °

Jerry is the son who was burned severely in the gas explosion when he was 18 months old. He shows few signs of the accident. His skin looks almost perfect. He is a husky fellow, an extrovert.

"I love my father," he said. "I really respect the man. I know he loves me too. Unfortunately, we're unable to say that to each other. I don't know why, even though I'm studying psychology.

"Dad always did a lot for us. He took us around with him

whenever he could. But we missed the one-on-one relationship.

"I'm a junior at Florida Tech, in Orlando, Florida. I need 48 credit hours to graduate. I also work for a wealthy invalid in a nice suburb there. He's in a wheelchair and I help him get around, get in and out of the car, things like that. I live in his house and get paid $75 a week besides. The man still works as a consultant.

"I resented my dad when I was 18 or 19. Now I understand we live in a world where everybody has to go out and make a buck. The best way for dad to do it was by traveling and making music. He would go out of his way to give us everything.

"Dad is a capitalist and usually the only way you can make it as a capitalist is by hurting people. But my father was different. He didn't hurt anyone. He's a beautiful person. He's enjoyed people who are rich and he's enjoyed people who have no money. He's helped a lot of people.

"I love my mother and I have five brothers who all love each other. I know if anything ever happened to me I'd have five brothers coming to Florida to help me. And if anything happened to them, I'd come to help them. How many families can say that?"

• • •

Andrea is a reserved, pretty girl. We wrote to her and asked her to summarize her feelings about her family in a letter, but there was no reply. When we phoned her, she explained that she was reluctant to say anything because she didn't want to hurt anyone's feelings.

"Ever since I can remember, my parents argued," she said. "I hated it. When I was little, maybe seven years old, I used to tell my sister that I wished they were divorced rather than have them argue like that. I couldn't stand listening to them and I'd leave the room. I left home when I graduated from high school and went to a business school in Chicago. I always said that if I got married, and was unhappy, I wouldn't stay with my husband.

"I believe my parents loved each other, but they couldn't get along. They always argued in front of other people. And they would always talk against each other to us kids.

"Dad would tell us about the things mom was doing wrong and I'd believe him. Then I'd be friendlier to him than I was to my mother. Then mom would tell us what dad was doing wrong and I'd turn around and be friendlier to her. This was bad, because I wanted to love them both.

"My parents wouldn't criticize each other for anything important. It was always over little, nitpicking things. One of the worst things parents can do to their children is pick at each other in front of them. It mixed up the kids. I've had problems myself. I've had professional help. I'm glad to say I'm fine now.

"I wanted a career in singing, but I always said my personal life was more important. I was determined not to let any career get in the way of that. I sang for a little while, with my brother Frankie as my manager, but I wouldn't put up with making any sacrifices. If I had a date with a boy and it was necessary to call it off to perform as a singer, I would forget the job and keep the date. Because that's how it starts. Before you know it, you're putting your career ahead of everything.

"Dad was always generous to me. He bought me all kinds of things, but that was the only way he expressed his love. It was hard for dad to understand why we couldn't talk to him. I became afraid of him.

"I would want to sit down and talk to him about normal, everyday things about growing up. But he always had business on his mind. I always felt he was preoccupied with other things. I'm still a little afraid to talk to him, but I'm much better.

"The situation is so much improved now, for all concerned. I couldn't be happier in my marriage and I'm working as a part-time librarian in an elementary school. Since I'm married I'm 100% closer to both my parents.

"Dad comes to our apartment now and stays overnight. Years ago he couldn't do that. He'd drop in, say hello, and then spend the night with friends. Now he comes over and relaxes and sleeps late. He'll never know how great that makes me and my husband feel.

"When we were young, we weren't allowed to sleep in. He'd really get mad if we slept until 8 or 9 in the morning. So it's nice to see that he's unwound some too.

"Pat is exactly what dad needs. He has a deep need to stay young and she's perfect for him. She's young and vital and beautiful. Mom has what she wants too. I lived with her and her new husband for about a year before I got married. I'm very happy for both my parents."

• • •

Johnny Yankovic talks matter-of-factly about his family relationships and seems to have little hostility. He is straightforward and phlegmatic.

"I don't go along with the idea that dad gave us things because he wasn't able to show us love and affection," he said. "When we were kids he gave us plenty of affection. He was really good at it. But as you get older, it's tougher to do that. You can't kiss a teen-aged boy, so you give him something he can make use of.

"Do I like dad? Listen, I'm 23 years old and even today I won't smoke in front of him because I know he doesn't want me to. Next week, as soon as he gets back from Hawaii, me and my wife Beth are going to invite him over for dinner. I want to get to know him better. I like him and respect him.

"When I was younger, dad was always rushing. He'd come home from the road and rush to talk to us. That made us rush. I know now that he was only rushing to give us a good life.

"When I was in the fourth grade I wasn't doing good in school, so I was sent to a psychiatrist. That was all baloney. I didn't need a psychiatrist. All I needed was my father. Somebody gave them this quack idea.

"If I wanted to, I could have been successful in school. I know I could have. One time I proved it. Dad sent me to the Valley Forge Military Academy in Pennsylvania, and I did really well. I just did it to prove to dad that I could get good grades. But I only stayed there one year. I felt penned in. I got homesick.

"I also went to four other high schools, St. Joseph, Cathedral Latin, Brush High and The Cleveland School of Friends. I still need a half year of credit for my high school diploma.

"I left home when I was 18. I had a girlfriend in Cleveland and she moved with her parents to Orlando, Florida. So I moved there too. We broke up later, but I stayed in Orlando and worked as an electrician's apprentice.

"Then my brother Jerry and I started a landscaping business in Orlando. Dad loaned us $4,000 to get started. We bought all the equipment and had four people working for us, but it didn't go. There are too many people living on social security in Orlando and they couldn't pay that much.

"Now I'm working as an x-ray machine repairman. After Beth and I got married, I bought a house with the help of my brother, Frankie. He had been in the army, so he was able to get a Veterans' Administration loan for me, and I bought the house. It's actually in Frankie's name. I have great brothers. We're all close and we all help each other if we can.

"I know I could have asked dad for the money for the down payment on the house. But I didn't want to. He's helped me so many times I didn't want to ask him again.

"Beth and I were really doing well until she got laid off, by the way. Now she can't get another job and things are a little tight. I make $112 a week clear, but our mortgage payments are $230 a month. With all my other bills, we're living on about $20 a week. I think we're going to have to apply for food stamps.

"It was a shock when dad got married again, even though we all knew Pat. She was our housekeeper and guardian and we always had good times with her. She would play baseball and hide-and-seek with us. I like Pat. We get along.

"I get along with my mother too. Last Thanksgiving we went to her house for dinner. Me and Beth went, and we took my brother Frankie's two-year-old son. He sat on my lap and I let him drive, just like dad used to do with us. My mother's new husband is a nice guy.

"As I said, all my brothers are close. Last night I was bowling with Robbie and Mark. Mark is a nice guy, and he's smart, but I'm worried about him.

"Mark's basic problem is that he's not living at home. If dad and Pat and Mark could get into some kind of agreement where they could live together in peace, it would be the best thing that could happen to him."

* * *

Robbie is the last of the Yankovic sons living at home. He has a vertical, one inch scar on his lip as a result of his car accident. He is a serious, introspective young man, in search of himself.

"I respect dad so much it's ridiculous," he said. "He knows how to make people happy and he doesn't do it just for money either. It's his life.

"I know dad wants me to play the banjo in his band, but I don't feel I'm good enough. When you're playing with The King you have to be good. People tell me to take advantage of the fact that he's my father and get into his band. But I don't think that's right. There are a lot of musicians who are much better than me who aren't making it because they don't have the right connections.

"I'm working now as a plumbing inspector's aide. It's a good job, but I don't think I'll stay in it forever. I'm very confused about what I want to do. I'm taking a course in accounting at Lakeland Community College, but books don't seem to turn me on either. The more I think about it, the more I want to get into music.

"I had a rock band when I was in the seventh and eighth grades. Sometimes I want music so bad that it hurts me when I see people playing. I want to be up there on the stage. But I'm self-conscious. I was born with a slight paralysis of the right side of my face and I'm afraid to smile.

"When I loosen up I know I have the talent. I have a few drinks and then I don't care what anybody thinks and I go up there and do it. That's what happened when I played at Johnny's wedding.

"A lot of people might think I'm spoiled, but that's not true. None of us were spoiled. Sure, dad gave us everything, but we had to work for it.

"Dad taught me how to do everything around the house. He showed me how to fix the light, solder iron, install sprinkling systems, anything and everything. He knew how to do all the work around the house and he wasn't afraid to do it.

"He encouraged all of us to go out and do things. Us kids ran all kinds of businesses in the neighborhood, landscaping, cleaning gutters, painting houses, plowing snow. When dad had the restaurant we worked as dishwashers and bus boys.

"Trouble is, dad wanted a perfect family. He wanted us to live up to an impossible ideal. If we did something wrong, he would cut us down in front of his friends instead of calling us aside. We became afraid to do anything for fear of making a mistake and being jumped on. I think I'm still like that now. When dad would come into the house we'd all jump and start doing things just to look busy.

"Dad always taught us to treat people well, and we did. But we had traffic through our house all the time. Sometimes we had so many visitors I'd want to whack them in the head, but we had to be nice.

"Frankie, my oldest brother, tried to be like a father to us when dad was away. He would get all the kids from the neighborhood and arrange football games in our yard, things like that. But then dad would come home. If he didn't like the way Frankie was running things he'd put him down.

"Pat says I shouldn't live in the past, but my past is part of my life. I've already lived 25% of my life, so how can I forget it?

"The worst thing that happened was when my friend Claude was killed in the car accident. When I heard he died I headed for the window. They grabbed me to keep me from going out. Me and Claude were so close. I think about him all the time.

"I looked up to Claude. He could put your mind in a state of relaxation. He had it all down perfect and everybody loved him for it. His big talent was arranging to bring people together. He would get 15 or so of us kids and we would drive into the country, take our guitars and just have a good time.

"After Claude died, Mr. Tanner, his father, told me to feel free to come and talk to him anytime. I went to see him a lot of times, but then I broke away because it hurt me every time I saw him."

* * *

Richard is sophisticated, witty, mildly arrogant. A top Chicago hairdresser, he lives with a friend in a beautiful apartment. He makes good money, but says he never is able to save any. He doesn't own a car.

"I was very close to mom and dad," he says. "I understood him and never had a problem talking to him, as some of the other kids did. That's because I have a habit of discovering a person's Achilles Heel and working on it.

"What's dad's Achilles Heel? He's a very lonesome man. He never found the one great love that he was looking for. So he converted his love into entertaining. That's why he's a great entertainer. He's very deep, sensitive, an artist.

"Dad is his own best friend. An entertainer has to be. He's not easily entertained or amused and it's very difficult for him to slow down and listen to anybody. That's why Ann Birsa is his closest and truest friend. She can talk to him and he listens.

"His head is always going and he can't sit still. This is good. People like that are fantastic.

"Another reason I got along with him was that I was smart enough to say no when he wanted to give me something. My brothers and sisters were dumb and said yes. He got it in his head that everyone was using him.

"One Christmas all of us kids got together and decided to chip in and give him some money. We collected about $125 and gave it to him in an envelope.

"He gave us our presents at the same time – $1,000 for each kid. It was kind of embarrassing, but amusing. Even dad laughed about it.

"We used to get all kinds of weird phone calls when dad was on the road. They would come anonymously, in the middle of the night. A voice would tell us dad had just been found murdered, or that he was in bed with somebody.

"When mom disappeared I lay awake nights trying to figure out where she was. I'm imaginative and everything went through my head. I heard the rumor that dad had buried her under the pool. It was difficult to work while she was missing.

"Finally one day, when I was working in the salon, she called me. As soon as I heard her voice, I said, 'Where the hell are you?' It disrupted everybody. All the customers heard and turned around to look.

"I was the first one she called. I think she called me because she felt she'd get a calmer, more rational reaction from me. I knew where she was for about three weeks before anyone else found out.

"She made me promise to keep her whereabouts a secret. She said it was the only way she could get a divorce. She was weak, a typical woman. She figured that if dad found out where she was he would talk her into coming back.

"I kept quiet for weeks, but then I told her that I would tell dad where she was if she didn't. I gave her two days to do it. Then she was found.

"When dad and mom split I was just as confused as everyone else. But it's turned out well for both of them. Mom's new husband is a kind, innocent guy. He's good to her.

"We were always taught at home to get out into the world and make something of ourselves, so I left home at 17 and went to a beauty school. Dad paid my way and I quickly got a job in a top salon.

"I found it difficult to study in school and quit in the 10th grade. But I was a straight A art student and took lessons in piano, modern jazz, voice, ballet and tap dancing. I studied dancing for 12 years.

"I had some problems when I was about 17 and went to see a psychiatrist. But he was a total fool and I walked out on him. I don't like Cleveland either. I avoid it whenever possible. If dad lived elsewhere I'd see a lot more of him.

"I wanted to go into the theater, but I like to eat. Show business is too rough."

CHAPTER XIII

PAT

For about a year after June left, I lived the life of a bachelor father. Not to pat myself on the back, but a lot of women wanted to latch on to me. I'm not kidding myself. I know I'm no Robert Redford, but I do have a certain amount of prestige and I earn a good income. Besides, I'm a nice guy. Many a woman thought of me as a good catch. In fact, I got propositions galore.

There was a secretary who came after me real strong. She was about June's age and had been June's girl friend. So she knew everything about me. I guess June had told her all the stories.

This secretary was a very smart girl and very religious too. But I never considered her as a possible wife. She just wasn't my type. But she did do a lot of typing and secretarial work for me.

As she got to know me better she started telling me how June had done wrong by me and how she had always liked me and wanted to go out with me. She was trying to soft soap me and I let her do it. But it wasn't getting her anywhere. I had no romantic interest in her whatsoever.

One day she told me that the members of the company she worked for were going to Boca Raton, Florida, for a convention. She said she thought she could get me a job playing at the convention, and that my air fare would be paid there and back. I accepted the job, naturally. As a professional musician, I'll play anywhere.

The trip to Florida came the day after I was honored as Slovenian Man of the Year in that big doing in Cleveland.

We celebrated at that party until 4 a.m. and I had to be at the airport at 6:30 a.m. to catch the plane to Florida.

When I got to the airport the secretary was waiting for me. She tackled me right there and wouldn't let go. She had made her mind up that she was going to be in control. She laid out a schedule she had made up for me. I had to accompany her to a banquet here, a dinner there, a meeting at some other place.

I went to a few places with her, just out of courtesy, but then I had enough. She didn't show any signs of loosening her grip. Finally I said to her, "Wait a minute. I appreciate you getting me the job, but that doesn't mean that I have to go everywhere with you."

She said, "What do you think I brought you here for? I want to be seen with you. I'll look like a fool if you're not with me after all the trouble I went to to get you here." I told her I was sorry and dropped her right there.

There were a few other women too, but not as many as you would suppose. Everybody always thinks that when they see me out with a woman that we're having an affair. Maybe that's the way kids think nowadays, but I'm old fashioned. I have to be real honest and say that there had to be quite a lot between me and any woman before I got intimate with her.

I met Pat, the girl I later married, at the steak house I had bought in 1965. Pat was working as a secretary then and she would come to the restaurant for lunch with her girl friends. She knew my partner, Jimmy Jerele, and one day Jimmy asked her if she'd like to work at our place as a combination bookkeeper and waitress. She accepted.

When Pat was hired she had never met me and didn't even know who I was. She wasn't interested in polkas and never heard of me. Also, since Jerele had hired her, she assumed he was the boss of the place. I had begun to cut down on my traveling by then but I was still on the road on weekends. During the week, I worked at the steak house, entertaining, tending bar, cooking and doing everything else. I can cook almost as well as a chef, by the way.

The first time I ever saw Pat was one afternoon after I'd come home from a trip. A friend of mine was celebrating his birthday in the steak house and I played and sang a few songs for him.

Pat took a look at me and asked one of the other waitresses, "Who's that?"

The waitress said to her, "Don't let him hear you say that. He owns this place."

After I met Pat, I was interested, naturally. She looked good but I wanted to see what she was like before I made any kind of move.

I'd watch her as she worked in the restaurant, trying to see how she acted with the customers. I wanted to see if she played up to them. I can't stand phony people. I liked the way she handled herself. She was friendly but businesslike.

Later I found out Pat was worried about the way I was studying her. I was so intent on watching her that I guess I stared at her with a kind of sourpuss look, never smiling. She thought I was watching her in the hopes of catching her if she made any mistakes. She told me later that she thought I was somebody she should avoid. I scared her. She liked the job and wanted to keep it.

Little by little we got to know each other. I found out that her name was Patricia Soltese and that she was 23 years old. She had always lived in the Euclid area, around East 200th Street, and she had gone to Euclid High School. She had been married briefly when she was 16, and she had a son by that marriage.

I also noticed that a young man would come to the steak house to visit Pat nearly every afternoon. They seemed to be friends. You could tell the young man was interested in her. This bothered me more than I cared to admit.

One night after the bar closed I asked Pat if she would like to join me and a group of friends for breakfast. She agreed. We had a nice time and afterward I got a little amorous with her. Pat got out of my car angrily and drove home. She said she had heard I was a Casanova. The next day I called her into my office and apologized.

After a while I asked her if she would be interested in doing some extra work at my house. I was having the house redecorated and there was a lot of work to be done, scrubbing walls and floors. In addition, I needed somebody to cook and clean for the kids while I was out of town on weekends. This would all mean extra money for her.

Pat accepted the job and she and her little boy moved into the caretaker's house I had behind the main house. She still had the job in the steak house, but before long she quit that and devoted all her time to taking care of my house.

It was at this time that we started caring for each other, although I want to emphasize that Pat wasn't my girl friend or mistress or anything like that, as a lot of people were gossiping.

One real bad incident took place during that time. It involved a Cleveland musician, whose name I can't mention. It would destroy his family. He is a supposedly happily married man.

It happened one day when I was on the road and Pat was home alone. This fellow came to the house and tried to make advances to Pat. He told her that she was a sucker and that I was just using her to keep up the house. He said she was making a big mistake and that I'd dump her when I got tired of her. All the while he was saying this, he was trying to grab her and kiss her. Pat kept pushing him away, but then she got frightened and ran for the bathroom and locked herself in.

The man pounded on the door and then he started to kick it. Fortunately, Robby came home just then and the man left. Pat called me in Lake Tahoe, where I was playing a six-week engagement at Harvey's Wagon Wheel, and told me what happened.

I phoned the musician and warned him to stay away from Pat. I didn't want to hurt his family, so I didn't press charges or tell his wife. But since then we don't say two words to each other. The guy played some jobs with me, too, but he'll never play for me again.

Pat and I had been talking almost every day on the phone during that trip, so after the incident I suggested to her that it might be a good idea if she drove the kids out to Tahoe for a little vacation. She agreed and set out with Robby, Mark, John, Jerry and her son, Greg. They drove to Tahoe in two and a half days and when they arrived a day ahead of time

I gave them hell for going so fast. I had told them to take their time because I didn't want any accident.

I have to admit I was mad for another reason too. I had a girl friend with me at the time. She was from Arizona, where she worked in a department store. She had been married and was a sensible, middle-aged woman.

She was discreet and wasn't going with me just to be seen. She really liked me. In fact, she didn't want anybody to know about us. She would write to me from Arizona and when she had a chance she would visit me wherever I was playing. She would buy my kids all kinds of presents too. I would tell her their sizes and she would pick them out in her store and wrap them up. She had brought several gifts to Tahoe.

Naturally, I didn't want to do anything to embarrass her or spoil her vacation. That was why I yelled at Pat for coming in early.

When Pat found out about the woman, she almost went home right away. That was when I began to see she had some real feelings for me. I, of course, had already begun to think that Pat was going to be more and more important in my life.

That evening I took a party of about fifteen people to dinner, including Pat and the woman from Arizona. I was trying to play it cool and not show any partiality toward anybody, so I sat next to some other people, not the women.

But then I had a few drinks. As the night went on, with everyone having a good time, I started to get playful. I tossed some grapes across the table at Pat and I reached over and put celery in her ice water, just like a kid. Then I went over and sat down next to her. That did it. The woman from Arizona left the party and went home the next morning.

A few nights later Pat and I came to a decision. We went into the coffee shop at Harvey's Wagon Wheel and had a heart-to heart talk until four in the morning. Pat pointed out that she had been taking care of the kids for several months and she said there was no future in that for her. She wanted to know what she had to look forward to, and she told me she thought the world of me.

I told her that I thought I would never marry again after June left, but that I needed help with the kids. I couldn't keep going on the road and leaving them alone. I told her I thought a lot of her too, but that I was afraid of the age difference between us. I told her I thought maybe it would just be better if I hired an older woman to be my housekeeper.

We kept talking it out and finally we agreed to get married. We decided to do it right away.

We made the six-hour drive to Vegas and were married in an all-night wedding chapel on the strip. The chapel was one of those places where they charged you extra for everything. An artificial corsage cost $50, and we had to give it back after the ceremony. Organ music was $20, and we hired a best man and a maid of honor off the street for $20 apiece. We thought it was all real funny.

After the ceremony they asked us if we'd like to celebrate with champagne and a shrimp cocktail. We took that too, for another $20. They served us champagne in a little plastic whiskey glass. One mouthful and it was gone. The whole wedding cost almost $200. The date was June 28, 1969. Pat was 24 and I was almost 54.

Funny thing, but Al Jalen was almost my best man for the second time. I had invited him to go to Tahoe with me before I left, suggesting a little vacation. Al wanted to come, but he couldn't make it. If he had, I undoubtedly would have brought him to Vegas with us so he could be the best man again. That would have been one for Ripley.

Pat and the kids stayed in Tahoe for two more days after the wedding, during which time we kept the news secret. I really don't know why we didn't tell anybody, except that I didn't want to get the kids excited and take a chance on ruining the vacation. I was afraid they might resent my getting married again.

Pat broke the news to the boys as they were driving home together. They took it well enough, except for Mark. He said, "I think dad married you to get revenge against my mother."

We had to get over a few rough spots when we were first married. I was aware of some of the talk that was going on. People were calling Pat a gold-digger and making other remarks like that. I could hear the whispers. But I think she's convinced everybody by now that she is a good wife.

Our age difference caused some embarrassing moments too. I would take Pat on a trip with me occasionally and some well-meaning old friends would say they were glad I had brought my daughter along. Then I'd have to introduce Pat as my wife. It bothered me but I never let anybody know it.

Pat had a couple of run-ins with June too. The first came one day soon after we were married. Pat went to visit Frank Jr. and his wife. June happened to be there, visiting from Michigan.

She glared at Pat, who pretended to ignore it and kept up a nice conversation. But June kept glaring. Then she said, out of the clear sky, "Frank Yankovic is the laziest son of a bitch that ever lived."

Pat defended me angrily. She said, "He is not. He's a fantastic guy. I've never seen anybody work as hard as he does." June kept arguing. She leaned over the table and raised her arm as though to hit Pat, whereupon Pat left the house.

The next day June called Pat at our house and told her she'd be sorry she ever married me. "You'll see how hard it'll be to live with him," she yelled. "His friends will destroy your marriage. None of his friends are any good."

Another time Frankie Jr. brought June to our house. June asked Pat if she could see the house for old times sake, and Pat said she could. June walked through it and looked around, then burst into tears. Pat had a lot of company that day and several people were at the pool, so June went out there. I made a phone call from out of town and June picked the phone up. But I wouldn't talk to her.

Since then, June and Pat seldom talk to each other on the rare occasions when they're together, because June always wants to get on the subject of rapping me.

Our biggest problem since we got married involved Pat's son, Greg. He is a nice fellow, but my sons just wouldn't accept him in the house. I guess they resented him and looked at him as an intruder. They were always picking on him. There were a lot of fights.

Pat was caught in the middle. On the one hand, she had to try to discipline the boys, but at the same time she couldn't seem to be showing any favoritism to her son. We didn't know what to do.

Finally, after about three years, we sent Greg off to live with Pat's married sister, Gail Witlicki, in Las Vegas. It was a hard thing to do, but I really think it was best for all concerned.

Greg, who is now 15, is doing beautifully in school in Las Vegas. He and Pat are always talking to each other on the phone. You ought to see those phone bills. I wouldn't be surprised if Greg gets back with us some day.

Right now my marriage is looking good. I've never been happier, without a doubt. I never knew what marriage was about before.

Pat is not a run-around type of girl. She loves to stay home with the kids, where June would get a baby sitter and go bowling.

Pat is very conservative. She buys a dress for $9.95. June would spend $125 for one.

I never enjoyed children like I do now either. Of course, I'm home a lot more now, maybe three or four days a week. I know my two kids now. Teresa hugs me and kisses me and jumps on my lap when I come home. Teresa was born June 19, 1970, and Tricia came along April 23, 1975.

Pat gets very upset when she hears people criticizing me as a father. She says I couldn't be a better father if I tried. She was here when my sons were still at home and she knows how hard I tried with them. She saw me bend over backwards to talk to them and try to get closer to them. She can't understand it when they say that I couldn't express love by giving them things. She blames June for not teaching them to respect me from the time they were babies. She also tells my sons it would be a mistake to go through life blaming all their troubles on the fact they come from a broken home. She says that's no excuse.

The major problem in our life together is my traveling. I take Pat with me as often as I can. She was with me, for instance, on trips to Alaska, Spain and Hawaii recently. But a lot of times my road work will get the best of her and she does some hollering. She says to me, "Why don't you slow up?"

The thing that bothers Pat most is that I'm not really at

home even when I'm home. She'd like to sit down and have a cup of coffee and talk, but I'm tied up arranging bookings and answering letters. I see a lot of people too, both for business and social reasons.

I have to entertain a lot. People are so good to me on the road that I tell them to look me up when they get to Cleveland. We have some great parties. I remember one where everybody was jumping into the pool with their clothes on. Pat likes those parties too. She is a gracious hostess. But sometimes we go for weeks with hardly any privacy.

But that's the nature of my business. I have to entertain people, whether I'm on stage or not. If I didn't they'd soon forget me. I'm not in show business only when I'm playing the accordion. I'm in it all the time.

Pat flares up sometimes and says it's a wonder that I don't have ulcers, since I'm always on. But that's one thing about me—when I get mad I don't hold it in. I throw it out of my system. I'll never have an ulcer.

About the only gripe I have against Pat is that she smokes. She's up to more than a pack a day now. I hate that. She promises she'll cut down, but I know she'll never quit. I don't know why, but I'm the only one in the family who never smoked. Seven of my eight children with June smoke. I tried to get them all to quit, but Linda is the only one who did.

People ask me if I ever worry that this marriage could break up too. Sure I do. It could happen very easily. Pat is too young to get tied down if she doesn't like the life. I only tell her one thing—if things are bothering you let's sit down and talk about it. Let's not start hurting each other without knowing what's going on.

I know that if we were divorced tomorrow we would still be friends. Pat often says this life is too tough on her. I feel sorry for her a lot of times.

CHAPTER XIV

FINANCIAL BOMBS

There was one more angle about my divorce from June that I haven't told you about. It had to do with money.

When June disappeared all kinds of thoughts went through my head. I was worried that she had left with some sharpie and that they were going to take me for everything. I just couldn't get this idea out of my mind.

So I took almost all the cash and stocks I had and gave them to an old friend to safeguard. The friend, whom I'll call Harry, manages his own company and I told him to protect the money so my wife couldn't get her hands on it in case of a divorce battle. He gave me a receipt for everything. If June would have come after the funds, I would have told the court that I had lost everything gambling. My friend had all the money hidden.

But the deal turned sour. June never came after me for anything and Harry never gave me back my money. He said his business collapsed and he was broke. I still don't know the true story of what happened.

Do I talk to Harry? Sure I do. I see him often enough. I figure there's no point in holding a grudge against him. What for? If he had to do what he did to me he must be in real trouble.

Besides, I figure I have to be nice to him if I'm ever going to have any chance of getting my money back. I'm hoping he can make a comeback some day and pay me. I know it won't do me any good to holler at him. Maybe it's the wrong theory, but it's my theory.

The only thing that bugs me about Harry is the way he handles his yard work. On occasion when I happen to be out his way I notice that he has the landscapers out, cutting the grass and trimming the bushes.

He's living like a plutocrat while I'm out there doing all my own yard work – and I don't owe a cent to anybody.

It's also ironic that I once had to pay Harry some money, and only because I was trying to be a nice guy.

A friend of mine had bought a night club in Superior, Wisconsin, and he told me he needed $4,000 real bad. He asked me if I could help him, so I called Harry.

I told him about my Wisconsin friend and suggested he talk to him. I told Harry not to loan him the money unless if he felt he was worth the risk. After he talked to him, he loaned him the $4,000. That was the last I heard of it.

But about a year later Harry called me and said, "Your buddy never paid me back the $4,000, so we're gonna go after you."

I didn't know what Harry was talking about, until he told me that my wife, June, had co-signed for the loan. I was on the road when the deal was made, so Harry came to our house and asked June if she would co-sign. She said, "Sure," and signed it and never told me. So when my Wisconsin friend didn't pay up, I was liable. I had to come up with the $4,000, plus $800 interest.

Those are just a couple of bad financial deals I've been involved in over the years. I can't complain. I have enough money, but I should have a lot more than I do. I blew an awful lot on bad investments. It was my own fault. Nobody forced me to put up the money. But I didn't get any help either.

I was too busy to think investments through because I was out of town almost all the time. So I had nobody to talk to about these things.

All of my investments were fly-by-night decisions. I would come home and somebody would suggest a get-rich-quick scheme that looked good. I'd say "Yes" and that was it. They never worked out. Not once.

I've always regretted that I didn't have somebody around who knew what to do with all the money I was making. I was earning more than I ever dreamed about, and I thought it was wrong to just let it sit there and collect interest. I figured I had to do something with it. But I didn't know what.

My attorney, Tony Trivison, tried to guide me a bit. He could have been a big help to me, but he never produced. He certainly meant well, but he didn't steer me the right way and let me get into bad deals.

To give you an example, in the 1940s Trivison advised me to buy $5,000 worth of stock in WERE radio in Cleveland. He was real close to the president of the station, which was a small one then. So I bought the stock and forgot about it. About ten years went by and I suddenly remembered that I still had it.

I asked Trivison about the stock. "What's the use of keeping it," I said. "It's not moving up. I might as well turn it in." Instead of talking me out of it, the lawyer sold the stock and I got my $5,000 back.

You can guess what happened. About two years later the station was sold for something like $6 million. I could have made something like $400,000 on the stock.

You can't really call that a disaster, of course. But it certainly was a missed opportunity, to put it mildly. I regret that he didn't have some knowledge of what was going on.

I blew another good chance in the early 1960s, when a friend suggested I buy the entire Ohio franchise of a new fast food chain that was featuring 15-cent hamburgers.

I asked Trivison what he thought and he said, "It sounds like a bad deal to me. Fifteen cents? What can you do with 15-cent hamburgers? You got to buy the bread. You got to pay the waitress. You got to buy the meat. What good is 15 cents?" So I refused.

That's how I lost my chance to get in on the ground floor of McDonald's Restaurants. If I'd gone in, I'd have so much money today that you'd need a computer to figure it out.

I've been burned too. Many times. One of the worst was when Fred Staup took me for $40,000.

Staup was a high-riding con man I got to know in the late 1940s. He was a tall, handsome fellow, about 40 years old. He had a wife that matched. She was blonde and slim and sang in night clubs.

Staup really impressed me. You have to remember that I

was only in my early 30s then. A lot of guys don't know which end is up at that age. Staup was always immaculately dressed and he was a great talker. He always seemed to have a lot of money to spread around too. He bet $100 on horse races and he shot golf in the 70s. He seemed like a guy who was always on top of everything. So, when he offered me a chance to invest in his finance company, I went in.

For a while, everything was beautiful. Staup was paying me 8% dividends regularly on my money. One day I went to my dad's house and waved a check at him. I had just been paid by Staup. "Look how easy it is, dad," I said. "You could get the same thing. Why don't you invest with Staup."

My father said, "You could wipe your ass with any receipts that you get from him."

But I stayed high on him. In fact, I made several radio and television commercials for Staup's firm. I'd play a few notes on my accordion and tell people what a great guy he was.

It wasn't long before Staup disappeared. He had taken in a lot of suckers like me and left with about $200,000.

The story made headlines in all the Cleveland newspapers for weeks. It was big news that Yankovic was one of the investors who had been fleeced. For several weeks Staup was the target of a police manhunt.

The federal men finally found Staup through his wife. She had gone to Detroit to visit her father and then she drove to Chicago. The G-Men trailed her all the way, right into a Chicago racetrack, where she met Staup. He was enjoying life, playing the ponies, as free as a breeze. He had only $288 in his pocket, though, when he was arrested and brought back to Cleveland.

What happened to the $200,000? Nobody knew. Staup filed for bankruptcy. Among his few assets, he listed four sets of golf clubs.

People were screaming for their money. One woman had given Staup $13,000 to acquire a hard-to-get liquor license. She didn't get the license or her money back. Another woman had given Staup $39,000 to buy a tavern. But there was nothing anybody could do. Staup said he was broke.

He was found guilty of embezzling in Common Pleas Court

on March 9, 1951, and was sentenced to one to 10 years in prison.

I wrote a letter to the judge, Harry Hanna, asking that Staup be put on probation instead. I offered to put him on my payroll as a publicity agent at $10,000 a year to allow Staup to make restitution.

My thinking was that Staup couldn't do any of us any good in jail. If he was working, he could earn some money to pay us back. Besides, I knew he'd make a terrific press agent, with his gift of gab.

But Judge Hanna turned me down. He said that the probation for Staup wouldn't be in the public interest. Too bad. I still think I had a good idea.

So Staup went to jail. He served for more than a year and a half and was released on October 8, 1952. I never saw him again. I know he divorced his wife a couple of years later. And there was a story in the paper once about him being arrested for running a floating poker game.

It's too bad about fellows like Staup. With their talent, they could make it big in almost any legitimate profession. But they want to do things the slick way.

I was always a sucker for friends. I've loaned a dozen guys money for projects that didn't work out. A lot of it went backing guys in saloons. The money just disappeared.

Once I gave two Italian friends, for example, $10,000 to invest in a plush little gambling joint in Cleveland. All I got for that $10,000 was two free meals. The place just didn't go.

A show business friend stuck me for about $45,000 in little dribbles. Over a period of four or five years I loaned him $5,000, then $10,000, then $5,000 again. I always had faith in this guy. Still do. He could be a real success but he always lived higher than his means. He'd always give me sob stories, that he needed the money for studio and office expenses. I kept lending him the money, hoping he'd hit big. I don't suppose I'll ever get paid, but we're still pals.

One old buddy got me involved in what was probably my wildest scheme. He suggested I buy an airplane and sell it for a quick profit. So I bought a 14-passenger Lockheed Loadstar plane for a very reasonable $6,000. This was around 1948. We went to Erie, Pennsylvania, to pick it up.

I thought it would be nice to put it to use once before selling it. I had a playing engagement in Hibbing, Minnesota, and we packed the plane full of people and flew them there with the band. It was a great trip. The whole town, including the mayor, was there to greet us when we landed.

I really felt like I had made the big time – traveling around the country with my friends in my own plane. We had a big polka jam session right there at the airport. Then we played our job and flew back to Cleveland. That was when the trouble started.

I should have sold the plane right away, because while we were on the trip the plane license expired. I knew nothing about plane licenses, but I thought it wouldn't matter. I'd pay the money and get another one, that's all.

But before I could renew the license, the plane had to pass inspection by the Federal Aviation Board. When they inspected the plane they found all kinds of defects. I spent $2,000 to fix something here, another $4,000 to fix something there. The bills kept going up. I had spent $20,000 and the end was nowhere in sight.

Finally I said, "Look, I've had it. Sell it." So I sold the plane for $2,000 in salvage.

The same guy who had talked me into buying that plane also stuck me later on. He had a used car dealership right next door to my old tavern on East 152nd. He asked me for $1,000 once and guaranteed me he'd give me back $1,100 in a few days. That's a 10% profit. I gave the guy the money and, sure, enough, a few days later he gave me back $1,100. This happened several times. The guy looked good as gold.

Then he told me he needed $10,000 real bad. He said he'd give me back $11,000 in a week. He had always come through before, so I gave him the cash. I never saw him again. I have no idea what happened. He just vanished from the face of the earth.

In 1965 I got into the steak house through Jimmy Jerele. Jimmy was an old friend who had worked in a lot of big restaurants around Cleveland, as a bartender and a maitre d'. He knew I was thinking of cutting down my travel a bit, and he suggested we go into the restaurant business together. Jimmy knew the business, so I told him to look around for a good location.

Milan Kapel, the builder, told us about a restaurant in a motel. I never saw the place because I was working in Nevada, but I told Jimmy to take a look at it. I told him that if he liked it, he should buy it. I gave him carte blanche. So Jimmy bought the place for $37,000. I put up all the money, as usual.

When I came home and saw how small the restaurant was, I was disappointed. It could only hold about 70 people. We had to break into six motel rooms to expand the place to seat about 175. I worked on it myself like a laborer.

That venture worked out all right. We kept the restaurant about eight years and made a nice living. We didn't get rich, by any means. But we had a lot of fun, lived well and I had plenty of food for the family.

The steak house was a gathering place for a lot of good spenders, including Cleveland's polka celebrities. The biggest night we ever had there was when Lawrence Welk brought his entire band in. He was appearing in Cleveland Public Auditorium (I did a few numbers in the show) and he came to my place as a personal favor to me.

People were standing five deep at the bar that night, just to see the champagne music maker. Lawrence didn't disappoint them. He signed autographs and he and his band members danced with the customers while my band played.

As Lawrence said in his book, he rarely went out when he was on the road, but he wanted to see my restaurant. His manager was against him coming, feeling he needed the rest, but he finally agreed when I said I'd have him in and out of my place in an hour. I tried to live up to my end of the bargain but Lawrence had such a good time he stayed until one in the morning. He even played the electric organ. (In his account of the evening in his book, Lawrence spelled my name as "Yankowitch." I still kid him about it.)

After about eight years there, Jimmy Jerele wanted to get out of the steak house. He had worked hard and I wasn't around as much as I should have been. The lure of the open road was still there. So I bought Jimmy out.

After that the place went down. The motel manager ran it in my absence. A few years back, I could have sold it for $100,000. Now the papers are going through for $20,000.

I got into another bad investment about three years ago. A guy I know sells mobile home trailers. He wanted to establish his own finance company, so he could handle his customers' mortgages himself. It made sense. Why give the money to the bank?

So he got me and another guy to invest $50,000 apiece in his finance company. Then the gas shortage came. That killed the mobile home business. My friend sold out and now we're getting our money back little by little. So far, I'm still $14,000 in the hole. But on top of that, don't forget, I've lost all the money I would have been making on interest if I'd kept the money in the bank. I've lost $10,000 right there.

When you talk about financial disasters, you have to mention one of my biggest – an $80,000 fire in my house in 1970.

I was playing in southern Ohio when I got a call that there had been a fire. I went home right away, driving all night, but I wasn't too worried. It didn't sound as though it was too bad.

When I got home at four in the morning I couldn't believe what I saw. The fire had started in the family room and kitchen, but almost every other room had smoke damage. We had to put new ceilings in every room. We had to replace all the frame work and woodwork to get the smoke odor out.

While the place was being repaired, my whole family lived at Kapel's Charter House Motel for six months.

I had plenty of insurance on the house, but they could never pay me for the things I lost that money can never replace. For instance, I lost my two gold records, "Just Because" and "Blue Skirt." The fire, by the way, was started by a short circuit in the wires.

Naturally, I'm sorry about the money I've lost, but I don't let it bug me. What for? It's gone. There's nothing I can do about it. The only thing that bothers me about it is my age.

Years ago I could afford to lose $50,000. I'd just work a little harder the next year and make it up. But now I'm a little too old for that. Anything I lose now, I'll never get back. So I don't invest any more. I made up my mind.

If I had to do it over, I'd just put the money I made in a bank and leave it there and collect interest. Or I'd buy a piece of land. Land is almost always a good investment.

As it was, I never made a good score. Oh, I picked up $8,000 once in a stock, but that was chicken feed compared to what I've lost.

Thank God I'm well fixed. Am I a millionaire? By no means. I wish I was.

CHAPTER XV

THE SHOW GOES ON

Etta Bogt is an 84-year-old widow who lives in Butte des Morts, Wisconsin. Whenever she feels a little sick or depressed she plays one of my records. She says I'm better than any doctor. Etta has been writing letters to me for about 15 years. She always includes a self-addressed, stamped envelope, to make it convenient for me to send back an answer.

Etta worries about me. She tells me not to put too much salt on my food so I won't get high blood pressure, and she warns me not to eat in cheap restaurants so I won't spoil my stomach. She also tells me to always wear white socks. She says the dyed ones are bad for your feet.

Recently, when we were playing near Butte des Morts, I thought it was about time that I finally met Etta personally. After we finished our job, we drove to Butte des Morts, looked up her house, and parked our motor home in her driveway. We slept in the motor home all night. In the morning, me and all the Yanks knocked on her door and surprised the heck out of her. She made us breakfast and we had a wonderful time until we had to drive to our next town. When we left, Etta said she hadn't had so much fun since her first grandchild was born.

I have friends like Etta all over the country. If it wasn't for them, I would have quit the road long ago. Some of them are so close to me that I consider them members of the band. When I come into their city, I have to stay at their houses. If I didn't, they would feel insulted. It's very seldom that I go anywhere now that I stay in a hotel.

Carl and Ann Birsa, of Chicago, for instance, just can't do

enough for us. They're probably my closest friends on the road. When we're in the Windy City, which is one of our favorite stops, we use the Birsas' home as our headquarters. I call Ann "daughter" and she laughs and says that I have mothers and daughters all over the country, taking care of me, doing my cooking and sewing. She says I've got it made.

The Birsas were the godparents for my youngest daughter, Tricia. They've been friends with most of my children and with both my wives. Ann and June still exchange visits today. My son, Richard, once lived for a whole year with the Birsas.

The Birsas handle a lot of my music business around Chicago too. People in the area who want to hire me call Ann and she takes messages and calls me at home to confirm any engagements. She also arranged a big Sunday magazine story the Chicago Tribune did on me in 1975.

Years ago I used to stay with Mr. and Mrs. Joe Ziomek in Chicago. Mary Ann Ziomek was Ann Birsa's best friend. After the Ziomeks moved to Arizona, we were invited to stay with the Birsas. As Ann says, "It used to be Ziomek's Hotel. Now it's Birsa's Hotel."

As a matter of fact, the Birsas' house is a kind of meeting place for polka musicians. Go there on a Sunday morning and you're liable to find four or five players stopping there for breakfast on the way to a job in another city.

When we're in St. Louis, we stay with Gene and Vickie Heckstetter and John and Ann Spiller. Spiller's the fellow who first brought me to St. Louis in 1951. He introduced himself and said he'd like me to play for his SNPJ Lodge 107 dance, provided our fee wasn't too much. I told him it was $500.

He said the lodge members might not want to go that high. Remember, that was 25 years ago. But then he said, "You come out and play. If they don't want to pay you the $500, I'll make up the difference out of my own pocket."

The Spillers didn't want to take any chances on the dance being a flop, so they went through the phone book at random picking out names that ended with "ski," "ich" and "vic." Any name that sounded ethnic. They told them all about the dance.

Spiller also drove around town with a big sign advertising my appearance on the top of his car. During the rush hour, he'd stop his car in the middle of the busiest intersections. He'd get out of the car and pull the hood up, as though he was having engine trouble. He wanted to give everybody time to read his sign. At the same time he'd turn up the radio so that a polka show that was on could be heard all over the street. While Spiller pretended to be working on his car, people on the corners would clap their hands and stomp their feet in time with the music from the car. When he would drive off, the people would cheer.

The dance, of course, was a huge success. Hundreds of people had to be turned away. Tickets sold for only $1.25, but people were waving $5 bills at the door trying to get in.

That set the pattern for us in St. Louis. For several years we had bookings at the Casa Loma Ballroom, where we would play from Tuesday through Sunday. One of Spiller's lodge members, John Biskar, wrote the "St. Louis Polka," and we recorded it. Mayor Raymond Tucker hung the record on his office wall.

The crowds have continued there ever since. In January 1976, Lodge 107 celebrated its Silver Anniversary of dances with Yankovic. It was in the Electrical Workers Hall and 780 people squeezed in. All the women wore silver tiaras and the men wore silver bow tires. The dance was a sellout and many checks for ticket orders had to be returned.

I gave Ann Spiller quite a scare once, by the way. I was staying at her house when I got a pain in my chest. Ann insisted I had to go to the hospital. She called an ambulance and they made me lie down on a stretcher. I was carried into the hospital. When they examined me they said I had heartburn. I played that night.

Joe and Josephine Prunk brought us to Denver for the first time. We used to play in their night club for eight weeks straight. Pat and Margie Lombardi, really great people, put us up all the time in Denver. Mr. and Mrs. John Popovich, the managers of the Slovenian Home there, are also good friends.

Some of the other wonderful people who wine and dine us and treat us like their own are John and Ann Rebernisek, Milwaukee; Steve and Susie Swiderski, Minneapolis; Marcie and Leo Tastsides, Vallejo, California; Clara and Fred Walker,

Yankovic and his wife Pat.

Carl and Ann Birsa of Chicago, godparents of Tricia, Yankovic's tenth child.

Composer-arranger Joe Trolli collaborated with Yankovic on many songbooks and recordings.

The gifted Joey Miskulin, who has been making music with Yankovic since he was a small boy.

Yankovic entertaining fellow Clevelanders at the All Nations Festival on The Mall, 1976. (William A. Wynne Photo, Plain Dealer)

Yankovic and wife Pat, with children: Theresa (left) and Tricia, Nov. 8, 1976.
(William A. Wynne Photo)

The Polka King relaxes with his recording collection and momentoes.

Azalia, Michigan; Shirley and Jerry Hall, Toledo, Ohio; John and Angie Barrone, Sandusky, Ohio; Stella and Joe Billowitz, Ridgewood, New York; Mr. and Mrs. John Brezovec, Bethlehem, Pennsylvania; Mr. and Mrs. John Blatnick, Allentown, Pennsylvania; and Mr. and Mrs. Frank Schardon, Jamestown, North Dakota. I could go on and on.

I do most of my traveling these days in a mobile home. I wish I had one 35 years ago because it's almost ideal for the kind of work we do. The mobile homes I've been using sleep six and they have a stove, a refrigerator, TV set and shower. In the last few years I've had three of them.

I lost one in an accident in 1974. Dennis Birsa, son of the Chicago Birsas, was driving me and Joey Miskulin home from a job in Milwaukee. Evidently Dennis fell asleep. The mobile home went into a ditch and turned over. The body was totalled, but there were no windows broken. The engine kept running as we were lying there. We had to crawl through the ceiling to get out. Fortunately, nobody was seriously hurt. All I got out of the escapade were very sore ribs.

After that, I got a new mobile home for $26,000 and got very good use out of it. In two years I put 150,000 miles on it. A few months ago I bought a new one for $40,000.

Because the business has changed, I don't have just one band anymore. Today, the jobs are mostly from Thursday through Sunday. So I generally use musicians that live in the town I'm playing in.

Occasionally, some musicians from Cleveland will take a trip with me, but most of the time that's impractical. Most of them have steady jobs in factories. If I book jobs in Chicago on Friday and in Minnesota on Sunday that would mean they would lose work on Thursday and Monday because of the travel. They just can't afford that. It would be different if TV hadn't hurt the ballrooms. If we were still playing seven days a week they could quit their other jobs and stay with me full time.

Two Cleveland guys who travel with me more or less regularly are Joe White and Eddie Stampfl. Stampfl is a former mailman who retired early because of his health. He often comes with me for a weekend. He's as good an accordionist as they come, Johnny on the spot, and he's always ready to put on a good show. White, a banjo player and singer, is a bachelor and likes to come with me when he's on vacation.

I always invite the players' wives along on our journeys, by the way. And anybody else who wants to come with us is welcome too. The more the merrier.

Pat, of course, is always after me to reduce my traveling. I probably will, but I doubt if I'll ever retire completely. I just don't believe in it. I've seen so many close friends, prosperous, healthy guys, quit their businesses and retire, thinking they were going to enjoy life. They sit around with their grandchildren, or go on long vacations, or just loll around in the backyard.

In a year they look like basket cases. Then they realize that the retirement they were dreaming of all their lives is actually a living hell. In my opinion, if you quit moving and working you lose everything.

I'm not going to let that happen to me. I'm really afraid of living like that. If I do quit the road, I'll still have my hand in somewhere, even if it's only playing weddings and parties.

I guarantee you one thing: You'll never see me retire to some quiet little old folks village. No sir. If I ever hang 'em up, I'll move to a town like Vegas, where there's plenty of action. In Vegas, if things got too dead, I could always catch a show or go to the crap table, which is one of my favorite pastimes.

I've even toyed with the idea of making Vegas my headquarters. I could live there and work weekend jobs in that territory. I've gone so far as to send Pat to Vegas to look for a house to buy. But she came back empty-handed. She doesn't believe that I'd be happy away from Cleveland. She feels I have too many ties there, and I do. But my bread and butter is not in Cleveland. I seldom play there.

I would like to confine my playing dates to only two or three a week, but it seems like I just can't do it. It's amazing, but I'm getting more jobs now than I've had in years. And some of them are of the type I've never had before.

For instance, a few months ago, I was hired to sing in a church wedding in Azalia, Michigan. That was the first time that ever happened. I sang the "Hawaiian Wedding Song" and "I Love You Truly" as the bride came down the aisle.

A few months ago I played in the clubhouse at Northfield Race Track in Cleveland before about 2,000 people. We had a big polka dance right after the races ended. That was a first too.

And now I'm in the television commercial business. A Canadian record firm, K-Tel, is pushing polka records all over the U.S. and Canada. They hired me to do a 30-second commercial that is seen in major markets all over North America. I was dead tired when I made the commercial and I didn't have time to shave. They didn't even put makeup on me. I look like hell, but the commercial seems to be working. A few months ago K-Tel sent me a healthy check as my share of the royalties.

I still do most of the driving these days, and I guess I haven't changed much. White says I could have made a living driving a getaway car for bank robbers. He's amazed at the way I can maneuver the motor home in and out of traffic. If there's a quarter-inch somewhere, I'll make it through. Joe claims I never pay attention to red lights if I'm in a rush, but that's an exaggeration.

I still get pinched from time to time though, and when I do I make it a policy to just keep quiet and give the policeman all the information he wants. Half the time the cops will recognize me and let me go, after a stern lecture that I ought to be more careful.

White often gets upset because we rush around so much. We're always getting to a job just in the nick of time, which is what happened in Sherman, Illinois, recently. We got out of the mobile home, went into the hall, and began playing immediately. We got there with about one minute to spare. We couldn't help it. We had plenty of pals who wanted to visit us during the day in St. Louis, where we played the night before. I mean, you can't turn down a guy who asks you to come to his 30th anniversary party, can you?

Wherever I play, I carry six blouses. They serve as my band uniforms and all my side men wear them. I give them to the Yanks before the job and they give them back to me when the job is over. Then I give them to the men I'm using in the next town.

The blouses were my own idea. I always wanted a uniform for the band, but I wanted a certain type. I didn't want suits and coats and ties. I think that's too formal for a polka band. So I designed a blouse, with full sleeves. The blouses are tailor-made, but loose fitting, so that almost anybody can wear them. They are also made of nylon, so they can be washed and dried without the necessity of ironing.

Aside from my friends and my work, I have two passions on the road—sauna baths and dice games. There's nothing I like better than to go into a YMCA in any city and just spend an afternoon relaxing in the sauna. It gives me time to think and rejuvenate myself for the next job.

I discovered dice on my trips to Vegas and Tahoe a long time ago. By this time I have become a dice fanatic. It's a sickness, really, but I love it. I like the speed of craps. I don't do any other kind of gambling, because I don't have the patience. I suppose I'll never quit dice, even though I must be $20,000 behind.

One of my worst dice sessions came at Tahoe around 1959, when we were playing at Harvey's Wagon Wheel. The band was earning $2,500 a week and I spent a lot of time at the velvet table. I was about $4,000 ahead. After we finished playing on our last night, I told the boys I was going to give the dice one more shot. We already had the instruments in the bus and were ready to go to Elko, Nevada.

When I said I was going into the casino, Herb Eberle and Roger DiBenedict, two band members, gave me $20 each. "Make us a few bucks," they said.

Well, I don't believe in playing for a few dollars. I don't want to stay at the table forever. I want to win or lose fast. In the first minute that night, I lost a few hundred dollars. Then I started digging. I lost the $4,000 I was ahead, and kept losing until I was out another $7,000. I was busted. I had to borrow money to pay the musicians their wages.

Another time I was at Alladin's in Vegas. I was ahead, but then I ran into bad luck. I bet $1,800 and lost it on one roll.

If any number except seven had come up, I would have won. I lost another $1,800 on the next roll.

My wife Pat was with me that time, playing nickels in the slot machine. She was holding $3,000 I had won earlier. I asked her for it and then I lost that too.

I've won a few times, of course. In Vegas once I picked up $6,500. I could do no wrong. Everything I bet came up. However, like most gamblers I bet small when I'm winning and big when I'm behind. It should be just the reverse, but I guess it's human nature to try to protect your winnings when you're ahead.

I'm the type of dice player who likes to stay a few minutes at one table, then move to another one. I don't want to know anybody else at the table or talk to anybody either.

None of this kind of folderol would be possible if I didn't keep working, naturally. But times change and your way of making a living changes too. If you're smart, you adjust and survive.

In recent years, for instance, the polka tour has become a popular thing, and I've become something of a travel guide. Me and Paul Wilcox, the host of the Polka Varieties television show in Cleveland, have taken thousands of polka lovers on trips to Spain, Yugoslavia, Mexico and Hawaii.

The Hawaiian trip in particular, seems to have become something of an institution. About three times a year we fill a plane with about 300 people and off we go. I'm proud to say that we've never had trouble filling up one of our tours. I hope it's because people like me and because they feel I'll do my best to show them a good time.

Wilcox gets a kick out of telling people I always seem to be driving in from some faraway city just in time to meet the group at the airport.

When I get there, I feel it's my responsibility to entertain the travelers and be as sociable as possible. So I begin playing and singing as soon as I get to the airport, no matter how tired I am. When it seems like everybody's having a good time and the trip's off to a fun start, I'll say to Wilcox, "Keep 'em happy. I'm going to catch a little nap." I sleep for 15 minutes on the plane and I'm fresh as a daisy, ready to go again.

One time I was playing in a front seat in the plane and everybody crowded around to listen and sing. The pilot got on the intercom and begged everyone to move toward the back of the plane. It was getting nose heavy.

But it's the one-night stands I love the most. A lot of entertainers hate the constant moving, but to me there's nothing better than a one-nighter. I like the feeling of excitement, meeting old friends I haven't seen for a while.

We recently came back from one of our greatest trips ever, a 30-day excursion through the West. We had sellout crowds all the way. We played two straight nights at the German-American Club in Phoenix, for example, and you couldn't have gotten another person in with a shoehorn.

We even hit a city I've never been in before, El Paso, Texas. The people there named a horse race in my honor, the Frank Yankovic Handicap, at Sunland Park. I bet $10 across the board on the favorite and won $30.

A lot of Mexicans were at the Elks Club dance in El Paso that night and they couldn't stop shaking our hands. They said they never had such a good time. They gave all the Yanks big Western hats. We'll have to go back, without a doubt.

We had our usual amount of vehicle trouble on the trip. The muffler on the motor home acted up in Trinidad, Colorado, and we couldn't find a garage man to fix it. So I put on a pair of overalls and went underneath and fixed it myself.

Later, just outside Albuquerque, the motor home broke down and it cost me $300 to get it fixed. White said I'd have to sing a lot of "Jaz pa ti pa zidana marelas" to pay for that.

As the cavalcade went on, John Poelker, the mayor of St. Louis, and Robert Sabonjian, the mayor of Waukegan, Illinois, both gave me plaques. There's a funny story in connection with the Waukegan plaque.

We were playing a concert in a shopping mall there and the mayor came on the stage. I wanted to give him a big introduction, so I said into the mike: "Here's a person everybody knows." But I couldn't recall the mayor's name, so I whispered to him, "What's your name?"

The mayor got a big laugh out of it and told the crowd a story about me. He recalled that years before, Ara Parseghian, the famed Notre Dame football coach, was supposed to appear at an affair on behalf of underprivileged children in Waukegan. But bad weather kept Ara from making it.

So the mayor called me and asked me to substitute. I was already playing at a dance in Waukegan, but I accepted the job and brought all the dancers from the ballroom to the children's home. We had a great time. On top of that, Parseghian showed up later too.

I like everything about this road life, even the hard work. One day recently, for instance, we were at the Birsas' home and the boys in the band were surprised to see me get up early in the morning and go outside.

I took a ladder, a pail of water and some soap and cleaned up our motor home alone while everybody else was still asleep. Then I went inside and Ann Birsa gave me my usual breakfast of corn flakes.

When I'm playing, I try to live up to my reputation as the polka king. I don't care where I am, or how small the job seems to be. I have pride. I figure people are there to see me and I want to give them something more than they get from other polka bands.

My habit on all jobs is to play three straight hours, take a half hour break, and then come right back with a snappy half hour of music, and send everybody home happy.

A lot of musicians play for 45 minutes early in the evening, while a club is still empty. Then, when people start coming in, it's time for them to take a break. By the time they get back, half the night is over. Not me. I want to give the owners their money's worth.

Ask Frank Sterle, who owns a popular restaurant and club in Cleveland. He had me in there one Sunday night and he was amazed the way I played. No intermissions for three hours. Sterle said I was the greatest entertainer he ever had there. That's the kind of talk that makes me feel good.

In places like Vegas or Tahoe, you have to be a real showman. The people don't dance the polka there, so you could be the best player and it wouldn't mean a thing. I joke with the audience and 90 per cent of the time I do vocals. You have to be on the ball, go from one song to another with no hesitation. You have to keep talking, telling stories, and acknowledging celebrities in the audience, or you lose touch with the crowd right away.

I don't always play the same songs either. I keep my eyes and ears open and try to judge the crowd, give them what I think they want to hear. I'm lucky I have a good memory. Sometimes I'll go way back for a song, like "If I Had My Life to Live Over."

But I stay current too. I like to sing songs like "Please Release Me," and "Somewhere My Love." A song that Freddie Fender recently put on the top of the country western charts, "Before the Next Tear Drop Falls," is also in my repertoire.

I expect my side men to be ready for anything. I figure they're pros and I don't waste time telling them what song I'm going to play. I just start playing and the boys come in. I have two rules for my side men: No drinking onstage and no talking to each other onstage.

I try to get the audience relaxed and in the mood. I've picked up a few tricks along the way. Lots of times when I'm playing in a small club, I'll say, "Good evening, everybody. We're gonna have a good time tonight. But first I want you to stand up and shake hands with the person behind you." The people look around, and blush a little, but they do it and we're off for a lot of fun.

If people are timid and aren't dancing, I'll play a slow song to get them on the floor. Then, as soon as that one ends, I'll come right back with a polka before they have a chance to sit down. The more they dance, the better I like it.

If they're still too bashful and aren't dancing, I'll stop the music and say, "What the hell do you think this is? A concert? I'll buy a drink for the first couple on the floor."

People usually come up to me all night long as I'm playing. It's almost like a receiving line. They shake my hand, request songs, and exchange stories about old friends and old days. I sign autographs, pose for pictures with them and sell my records.

We almost always play to big crowds. For example, we performed in the Calumet Shopping Center in Chicago recently. They were running a series of shows, with different bands coming in each week. Herb Alpert and Count Basie were there before us.

When me and the Yanks came in, they had 4,000 seats set up. But a crowd of 8,000 attended. It was the biggest turnout of the series.

We were scheduled to do an hour show and we banged out one song after another. The people loved it. Then I gave the boys a breather. I introduced them all individually and told the crowd a joke about a little boy that drew a big laugh. The joke went like this:

This little boy told his mother he had to pee. His mother scolded him, saying, "Don't say you have to pee. That's not nice. Next time you have to go say you have to whisper."

The next night the little boy was staying at his grandpa's house and he said to him, "Grandpa, I have to whisper."

The grandpa said, "That's all right. You can whisper right in my ear."

When the little boy was finished, the grandpa said, "I'm glad you didn't have to shout."

The crowd really liked it. When they finished laughing, we swung into "Just Because," and "Blue Skirt." Then we played our international medley, made up of songs of various nationalities – Slovene, Polish, Spanish, German, Bohemian, Slovak, Italian, Croatian and several others. The show went so well we played an extra 20 minutes.

As this is written I have just come back from another great trip, a two-week journey that took me back and forth across the country and into Canada. I'll give you a play-by-play because it is a good example of how I live and work.

The jaunt began November 30, 1976, when I left Cleveland at six in the morning and drove to Chicago alone in my motor home. I had sold the motor home to an Alaskan and I left it with the Birsas. The Alaskan was flying to Chicago to pick it up. In the meantime, I flew to Winnipeg, Canada. Bobby Chick, my Chicago drummer, went along with me for the ride.

I hadn't played in Canada in 17 years. I was going up there in response to an invitation from Brian Sklar, who has a western country band that plays all over western Canada. The band is called the Western Senators. Brian had called me four months earlier, asking me to come out. I had never met him, but when he told me Joe Schultz was his accordion player I was interested. I knew Joe from the old days and I knew that if he was involved I wouldn't be stepping into something that wouldn't turn out right. Joe is a fine accordionist.

Chick and I arrived in Regina at 12:20 a.m. It had been a long day for me since I'd left Cleveland the previous morning. I was dead tired, but Sklar, Schultz and the rest of the boys in the band greeted us at the airport and I felt better. The boys were all cheerful, eager beavers, and I knew I would have a good time.

When we got into the customs area, I had to open up the two boxes full of records and tapes I had brought with me to sell on the tour. I had about 125 albums and 50 tapes. The border people were strict. They counted each and every record and tape. I was across the border many times in the old days but I never saw things that tight. I wasn't worried though. I wasn't trying to smuggle anything in. I paid the duty and went with the boys to our motel.

The next morning I went to CKCK-TV to see my old buddy John Sandison, the Morning Mayor, and appeared on his talk show. Then I visited Mayor Henry Baker at City Hall. He was the same mayor who used to have us at his house all the time when we played Regina in the 1950s.

I was really surprised that Henry was still the mayor after all these years. Politicians don't usually last that long. He said he lost one election but that he was voted back into office the next time he ran and stayed in ever since.

Mayor Baker talked about old times and gave me a pair of cufflinks and a Buffalo Bill hat. He also gave me a beautiful pin for my wife. The mayor said he was going to Hawaii in January and when I told him we would be there at the same time he asked me if I could introduce him to Don Ho, the Hawaiian entertainer. I told him I'd be glad to and that he should look me up.

After visiting friends like John Santalab and Luke Vancha, who owns a chain of music stores in Canada, we went to the Trianon Ballroom for the dance. Ross Sneath still owns it after all these years. In the old days Ross used to come up and play drums with us, just to be part of the show.

The dance that Wednesday night was like old times. We packed in about fifteen hundred people. Most of them stayed until the bitter end. We didn't quit playing until 1:30 a.m.

I didn't have time to walk around the ballroom the way I usually do because I had to stay near the stage and autograph the albums people were buying. They ate them up hog wild. I sold just about all the records and tapes I brought with me on that first night.

During the dance a guy I never knew before came up on the bandstand and insisted we come to his house afterward. I thought he was just a happy guy who was celebrating a little too much. But he kept insisting we visit his house. Finally we agreed to go.

It turned out the man was a retired industrialist. He owned a plant in Regina. The man, Roy Riche, and his wife Mary, laid out a big spread for us. We stayed until about 5 a.m. They made us sign their guest book and autograph pictures. It shows you what great people they have out there.

The next day we drove to Melville, Saskatchewan, where we played at a private affair at the Knights of Columbus Hall. It was an exclusive shindig for about 100 people. They had speeches and a beautiful dinner.

I was introduced as the featured guest, but I thought the people might be a little too high class to appreciate polkas. I was afraid they might not get up and dance. But when we started playing they liked us fine.

Immediately after the job we had to start driving to Edmonton, a 560-mile haul. We went in three cars and drove all night, getting to Edmonton at 3 in the afternoon.

We played the next two nights at the Red Barn Hall, about 30 miles outside of Edmonton. They were sold out both nights. The Red Barn management, in fact, warned people on the radio that they shouldn't bother coming to the hall if they didn't have tickets in advance. The hall held about 1200 people.

The Western Senators began playing first, then brought me on stage with a big introduction. From there on I sang almost every song. I sang Slovenian, modern stuff, everything. I sold out the rest of my albums and was kicking myself because I hadn't brought more. I felt bad about it because I knew people wanted my special 40th anniversary album.

When we finished playing Brian gave a speech to the crowd and I was presented with a trophy.

During our stay in Edmonton I got a chance to cut up old touches with Gaby Haas, the Canada polka star. He invited me to his Hofbrau Restaurant and I chatted with him and his young wife.

Gaby told me I was responsible for keeping him in the music business. He said he was going to give up music and give his accordion away about the time we first came to Canada more than 20 years ago. He said that after he heard my style he reconsidered and began playing again.

After we finished our job in Edmonton we got to bed about 4 a.m. At 7 a.m. Chick and I had to catch a plane for San Francisco.

We were met there by Leo Tastsides and his son. I was really tired but Leo coaxed me into accompanying him to the Hofbrau Haus there. Every city in the world has a Hofbrau Haus. As a favor to Leo I went, and played a little and talked to people. It was one of those times when you knock yourself out for an old buddy.

We stayed at Leo's house for two nights and he gave us his car to use when he went to work. I took Chick sightseeing. One place we visited was Pete Alioto's restaurant on Fisherman's Wharf. My friend Johann performs there, standing by the entrance and playing the accordion 12 hours a day. Johann said it was his birthday. We stayed for a few drinks and dinner.

The next day we flew to Los Angeles because I had to appear on Lawrence Welk's television show. We went directly to the Hollywood Palace, where the show originates.

When we arrived Lawrence was having his afternoon nap. His secretary, Laurie, greeted me and said, "Mr. Welk wants to see you as soon as he wakes up."

I was given a nice dressing room, which I shared with Myron Floren, the accordionist. Myron told me his daughter had just made him a grandfather for the first time the night before. She is married to Bobby, the dancer on the show. Myron was very excited.

I was at the Palace from 2 to 10:30 that night, rehearsing the show. I know most of the musicians and had some nice chats. Norma Zimmer, the Champagne Lady, gave me a warm welcome.

At one point during rehearsals I had lunch with the six Semonski sisters, the singing group. Their parents were there too. They are Polish and hail from New Jersey. Their dad said that he would like his daughters to sing with me on "Polka Varieties" in Cleveland sometime.

After Lawrence woke up, I went to see him. He said, "Frank, it's so nice having you here. If there's anything we can do to make your stay more pleasant just let us know."

I asked him what he wanted me to play on the show and he said, "Just Because." I had already done that on his show and was hoping to do something else, maybe a medley including "Moja Dekle." But it was too late. Lawrence said he had already told the band we would play "Just Because."

The studio was filled with about 200 spectators for the dress rehearsal. Then they cleared everybody out and brought in an entirely new audience for the actual show. They want the audience to be fresh and respond enthusiastically.

I did my number and also played with the band in another segment. Lawrence wished me good luck with my book. "Everybody's an author these days," he kidded me. Lawrence has had three books.

After the show Lawrence asked me where I was staying and I told him I didn't have any plans. He invited me and Chick to be his guests at his motel in Escondido. The motel is called Welk's Country Inn and it's located on Champagne Boulevard. It's a beautiful place, set away in the mountains. It has an 18-hole, par three golf course. Everything was perfect there. Paul Ryan, the manager, couldn't have been nicer for the three days we stayed.

Welk also rents out space for mobile home parking on the motel grounds, by the way. Business is so good that there's a two-year waiting period for people who want to park their mobile homes there permanently.

While in Anaheim we went to see old Cleveland friends Jean and Bill Sitter. They were tickled pink to see us. Bill used to be a printer for the old Enakopravnost, a Slovene newspaper, in the long ago.

Then we called the factory where I was supposed to pick up my new motor home. I had intended to drive it back to Cleveland. But I got the bad news that it wasn't ready yet. The dealer apologized for not making the deadline and said he would buy me an airplane ticket for the flight back to Cleveland. By that time some Cleveland pals, Al Jalen and Esther and Chuck Lampe, had joined us. They had come out for a small vacation and had also expected to drive back to Cleveland with me. So the dealer said he would provide airplane tickets for them too. In addition, he said he would have the motor home delivered to me in Cleveland when it was ready.

My old friend Joe Sonce of Detroit, who is now a car dealer in Los Angeles, got me a brand new Oldsmobile to use during the rest of my stay on the coast. We had a couple more playing dates to take care of. On Saturday we played in Van Nuys and on Sunday we were at the SNPJ Hall in Fontana. I was paired with accordionist Ed Tomazine.

On Saturday afternoon I visited the SNPJ old age home in Fontana. I went there specifically to see my old friend Frank Ciligoj, who is 71. Frank used to be a boarder in my parents' home. Years ago, when he was a young guy, he lost a leg in a motorcycle accident. He was turning a corner on Holmes Avenue in Cleveland when he crashed. My dad had taken him to the hospital the day of the accident.

Frank was a real Slovenian type. He liked to make wine and loved to talk and sing. But the years had taken their toll and when I saw him he looked good, but he was depressed. I asked him to come to the dance at the SNPJ Hall but he said, "No, no. I don't go out anywhere." I couldn't get him to change his mind. I said so long, and told him I'd be back the next day. Then I visited all the other people in the home. It is a nice place, not modern, but clean.

The next day, after visiting Joe Mlakar's Elbow Room in Fontana, I went back to the home again. I brought my accordion with me and I said to Ciligoj, "Come on, Cili. I'll play a couple of numbers for you."

I played and sang in the dining room for about 45 minutes. All the oldtimers listened. They were thrilled. In fact, they postponed their lunch until I finished playing.

When I ended I again asked Ciligoj to come to the hall with me. Finally he said yes. That night I sat him next to the stage with Jalen, who was selling my records. I dedicated some songs to Ciligoj and he smiled and cried every now and then. It was a touching experience.

The next day we began our trip back to Cleveland, with a short layover in Las Vegas. I called my friend Billy Weinberger, president of Caesars Palace, and he gave the Lampes, Jalen and me beautiful rooms. We stayed for a night and I did a little gambling. I won about $600 this time. Then we flew back to Cleveland.

But the next day Pat and I boarded a plane for New York, where Epic Records was holding a farewell party for an old friend of mine, Steve Popovich. Popovich had a Croatian tamburitza band in Cleveland about 20 years ago, and one day he asked me if I could fix him up with a job with Columbia Records in New York. I was recording with Columbia at the time.

I always liked Steve, so I told him I'd see what I could do. I talked to the regional manager in New York and he gave Steve a job as a stock boy at Columbia. From there he worked his way up until he became one of the company's top executives. Then he transferred to Epic, where he also held one of the top jobs. Now he was leaving to go into business in Cleveland.

The Epic people were throwing a $200-a-plate party for Steve and they asked me to entertain. The party was held at the Bijou Restaurant, a real high class place. There were about 100 people there.

Pat and I felt out of place when we arrived. We were the only ones who were all dressed up. Pat even had a gown on. All the other people at the party were dressed casually, wearing beards and levis. That's how everybody in New York looks.

The Epic people told me to make sure to get lost between

7:30 and 9 o'clock. Popovich didn't know I was going to be there and they wanted to surprise him. They even told me to hide my accordion. So me and my musicians went to the German Village restaurant. Pat stayed at the party and enjoyed herself. She said they served hors d'oeuvres that were out of this world while I was gone.

When I got back I surprised the heck out of Popovich. He embraced me and nearly broke into tears. His mother was at the party too. I told the audience the story of how I got Steve a job at Columbia and then we played and sang. It was a great night all around. Steve, by the way, looked just like all the other New Yorkers. He had a beard like Santa Claus.

We stayed in New York for a few days while I showed Pat around. She rode the subway for the first time, I took her to Sardi's Restaurant and to Macy's and Saks for some shopping. We even went to Greenwich Village to see if the Village Barn was still there.

That was the place where we performed in the late 1940s and early 1950s, and where Johnny Pecon played his last job with me. But it was gone. None of the people we talked to in the village had even heard of the place. Time flies.

Pat and I also saw three movies while we were there. That's something I rarely do, but I was in the mood for it. We saw "King Kong," which was very good, and a boxing movie, "Rocky." Don't miss that one. We also saw "Carrie," which I didn't like. Only the last 15 minutes were interesting.

New York isn't a good place to live anymore. Manhattan is like a wino section and all the stores have steel grates on the windows. You see people rummaging in trash cans looking for old food and something to drink. It's sickening. Around Times Square all you see are dirty movie theaters.

When we got back to Cleveland I went to the Holmes Avenue Slovenian Home, where disc jockey Tony Petkovsek was conducting an all-day radiothon for the Slovene Home for the Aged in Cleveland. All of the community's polka personalities donated their time and talents and listeners phoned in pledges. I played for the benefit and also contributed $100.

Just to show you how Slovenes take care of their own, let me tell you about a gesture made by John (Cookie) Kolovich, manager of the Slovenian Home club room. He donated all of the proceeds from that day's liquor sales to the old age home. And you know how Slovenes drink.

As soon as I was finished with my radiothon appearance, Joe White and I began driving to Avonmore, Pennsylvania, where I had another job that night. I didn't have my motor home yet and my car isn't big enough to hold our instruments and the sound system. So we borrowed Lampe's station wagon. We went only about 20 miles when it broke down.

I called Eddie Grosel and he brought out his station wagon for us to use. We were clipping along toward Avonmore when Grosel's wagon started giving us trouble too. It started backfiring and coughing and we couldn't go over 20 miles an hour.

We finally made it to the dance at 10:15 that night. We were supposed to be there at 9. The people were real glad to see us and to make it up to them we played overtime.

While we were playing we got a mechanic to work on Grosel's car. By the time we were ready to go back he assured us it was fixed. So we took off down the turnpike. Sure enough, the same thing happened again. The car started making noise. This time we couldn't go over 10 miles an hour. We finally made it home at 7 in the morning. I took the instruments out of the car and went to bed. But I knew I wasn't going to get much rest. I had to catch a plane to Milwaukee two hours later.

At 9 a.m. Lampe picked me up and drove me to the airport. Denny Boneck, one of my bass players, picked me up in Milwaukee and we drove to the Kloten Oasis, a beautiful spot, where we played from 2 to 6 in the afternoon.

We had a real good time there. Mary Ziegenhorn, a close friend who owns a tavern in Sheboygan, brought me some stomach (zelodec) and a Slovene delicacy called "flancete." Everybody had the Christmas spirit.

That night I stayed at Boneck's house and then at 6 a.m. I had to fly back to Cleveland. Joey Miskulin picked me up at the airport and drove me home. I went to bed dreaming of the nice receptions I got all over the country on this trip.

That's what gets me more than anything—when the people like us and appreciate our music. It makes me want to play and play. That's why I don't think I'll ever quit.

CHAPTER XVI

POLKA PEOPLE'S COMMENTS

NORMAN (FRITZ THE PLUMBER) MARGGRAFF, disc jockey, Milwaukee – "Yankovic is the only international figure in the polka world. He is the greatest promoter in polka history and his band is the most imitated in the United States, including the pop field. Nobody will ever touch him.

"Before Yankovic, ethnic bands stayed in their own little pockets. But then he came along and made polkas palatable to the general public. It was unheard of for a polka band to go to Las Vegas, but Yankovic did. Others tried, but they just don't have his business sense or charisma.

"He's made a big comeback lately. In the 1960s it looked like polkas were finished. But Frank stayed with it and now there's a renaissance and he's more popular than ever.

"I remember I was on a program with Li'l Wally and Frank about eight years ago and Li'l Wally heard Frank play and said, 'That poor old man has had it.' I said to him, 'Don't count him out.' Look at Frank now. He's going stronger than ever and Li'l Wally is in semi-retirement in Florida."

KENNY BASS, disc jockey, Cleveland – "Yonkee has foresight. He can look down a hallway and see around the corner. He was raised to be a businessman, to entertain people, and to be competitive. He always wanted to win. He grasped more than the others the importance of personal appearances. The man is brilliant. He would have been a success in any business he went into.

"When he started, it was unheard of for a major label to put out polka records. But then he broke through on Columbia and made it easier for all of us. It was like going from the minor leagues to the majors. All of a sudden Vadnal, Habat, Pecon and my band all had recording contracts with the big outfits. The interesting thing is that we were all Collinwood Slovenes who had grown up a few blocks from each other. None of it would have happened if it hadn't been for Yonkee.

"I had also been trying for two years to start a daily polka show on Cleveland radio and I couldn't get anywhere. Nobody wanted to take a chance. Then, after Yonkee made it on Columbia, they finally put me on. They figured I had a star act to play — Yankovic. In the first two weeks I was on the air I got thirteen sacks of mail. Twenty-seven years later I'm still on the radio."

FRANK J. LAUSCHE, former U.S. Senator, Washington, D.C. — "Yankovic made himself one of the great stars of the nation, a musical phenomenon. I saw him play frequently and always enjoyed listening to him, from the days when he was on the radio with Heinie Martin. My brother, Doc, held him in great esteem. They recorded many songs together, including 'The Cleveland Polka,' which Doc composed."

JOE TROLLI, arranger, Cleveland — "Yonkee is not the greatest player, but he has power. Some guys can play strong for an hour or so. They get drunk and go like hell, but then they peter out. But Frank can keep going with a lot of steam longer than anybody else. For a guy who's only 5-feet-8 and 160 pounds, he's strong.

"If it wasn't for him you wouldn't have all these polka programs on the radio like you have now. Before he came along polkas were nothing but sideline stuff. You'd hear them at weddings or little parties and that's all.

"A lot of Cleveland musicians are jealous of Frank, but it's mostly the older guys. They're jealous of him because they didn't get very far. What do they want? They take polka tours to Hawaii. That's not bad for guys who only had lessons for two years. Frank always treated me like a king."

ANN BIRSA, friend, Chicago — "Frank is the hardest worker I've ever known. He just keeps pushing, pushing to stay on top. His second love is the typewriter. If he has a day off, he has a cup of coffee and then you just don't see him again. He goes into his room and starts typing letters. He doesn't know how to relax. He never did and he never will. Once he sat down and watched television and fell asleep for five minutes. When he woke up he said 'Oh, my God, I got mail to answer.'

"I can't say if he's ever been sick, because if he was you and I would never know it. He's performed many times with a 104 degree fever. Some people say he gets mean if one of his musicians pleads illness, but that's not true. He just can't understand why one of his men can't keep going if he can. He thrives on pressure. If he didn't have it, I think he'd fall apart.

"The nicest thing about him is that he never forgets the average person. He got big and stayed himself. That's the nicest thing you can say about anybody."

JOHNNY SANDISON, disc jockey, Regina, Saskatchewan – "Frank would travel hundreds of miles all night, then come into town and be on my 'Morning Mayor' show at 6 a.m. No wonder he still holds the record attendance at the Trianon Ballroom here. Frank also played at the most unique dance I ever saw. Several patients from a hospital danced in their wheelchairs to his music. He had tears of happiness in his eyes. From Regina to New York he always was and always will be the Polka King."

DON SOSNOSKI, polka historian, Cleveland – "Yankovic is the man who made polka music what it is today. He is Mr. Show Business in the polka world. He bridged the gap between Slovenian and Polish music.

"There are only a few other polka bandleaders who have played as long as he has. Matt Hoyer, of Cleveland, had a lengthy career. He played from 1905 to 1958, but he didn't travel much out of town.

"Harold Loeffelmacher, of New Ulm, Minnesota, which used to be called the polka capital of the U.S., parallels Yankovic. He is now in his 70s and is still playing. But Yankovic out-traveled him by a long shot."

JOHN REBERNISEK, tavern owner, Milwaukee–"Frank's one of my closest friends. He gave me one of the trophies he got when he won all those polka king contests. There's nobody like him. I've seen him play for retarded children. There's something about the music they like. He gets them to join in on the singing, and he calls some of them up to play with him.

He'll hold their hands so they can play the electric organ. You can see how much it means to them from the expressions on their faces."

LUD LESKOVAR, disc jockey, Chicago – "He was the first to bring polkas out of taverns and into radio and television. He ended the prejudice against foreign entertainment on TV. He was ahead of his time. In those days there was a rush to get into the melting pot as fast as possible. Now people have the idea of maintaining their ethnic individuality.

"He played for us in the Bohemian Sokol Hall in Chicago right after his big accident. People said he couldn't play anymore, but there he was. What a thrill! He was in some kind of contraption and he didn't play much. But his presence was enough. He'll last a long time. He's from hardy stock. The place in Slovenia where his people come from, Kras, is very rocky and hard to make a living in. The people from there live a long time. They're tough."

JACK O'BREZA, JR., publisher, Polkarama, Cleveland – "You can't compare Yankovic with any other polka band. I went to Bowling Green State University and it was no use talking about bands like Bob Timko's or George Staiduhar's there. The only one they ever heard of was Yankovic's. Without him, polka music would be more localized. For instance, I have a friend in Scottsdale, Arizona, who never hears polkas except when Yankovic is there."

JIMMY MAUPIN, accordionist, Milwaukee – "I've had a few battles with him. Once he hit me on the nose. I got a date mixed up and didn't show for a job. Another time he walked into my tavern and asked me if I'd like to make a record with him. He said he'd put my name on the cover with his, equal billing. This was something he'd never done, so I asked him if he was kidding. He assured me he wasn't and we cut the record. I know why he did it. Because I have a 12-year-old daughter who's blind and retarded. He wanted to do something for us."

BILL SELES, disc jockey, Pittsburgh – "I firmly believe that without Frank polka music in the U.S. would be a pleasurable experience for only a limited number of people, those with strong ethnic ties. He was always ready to promote polkas by way of an interview or promo tape."

EDDIE GROSEL, disc jockey, Cleveland – "Once we were driving to New York. I was going 80 miles an hour and Frank was sleeping. Then he poked me with his elbow. His eyes were closed, but he said, 'Slow down.' He's been on the road so much he can tell from the motion when the car's going too fast. The fastest I ever saw him drive was when we took Father Perkovich from Cleveland to Valparaiso, Indiana. We had a flat tire. After that it was 90 miles an hour all the way. He had Father Perkovich and about 50 people from Minnesota at his house for Thanksgiving dinner, by the way."

RAY STRUMBLY, realtor, Cleveland – "We joined Yankovic once on a mystery bus trip. He filled a whole bus with people and off we went. We didn't know where we were going but we had confidence Yonkee would show us a good time. We went to Ann Arbor, Michigan, where Frank was playing at a place called 'Bimbo's.' We had a great time and then a retired Ford Company executive who was there invited the whole busload to his house. What a sight! At 2 in the morning this Greyhound bus goes rolling into this exclusive neighborhood. The executive's wife was a double for Sophia Loren, the movie star. The house was gorgeous. We had a ball. The next day Frank had to fly to Canada for another job, while we took the bus back to Cleveland to his house, where Pat had an all-day pool party for everybody."

TONY GRANATA, president, musicians' union, Cleveland – "Yankovic is a wonderful guy, one of the most famous citizens of our city. He's Mr. Big, but he doesn't act big. The mayor asked me if I could get Frank to play at our All Nations Festival, so I asked him. I knew he could get paid five times as much, but I told him we could only pay scale. The City doesn't have the money. He was glad to do it and has played for me everytime I've asked him. When President Ford came into town during the last election the White House guys phoned me and wanted to arrange a picture of Ford with Yankovic. When Walter Mondale, the vice president, came into town during the campaign the first thing he said at the airport was, 'Where's Frankie Yankovic?' "

BRUCE BURGER, disc jockey, Cleveland – "Yankovic is one hell of a man. You really have to respect him. He's one of the smartest guys you'll ever meet. It's impossible to win an argument from him.

"He's a victim of professional jealousy. There are a lot of professional musicians around, racking their brains, playing in small places, and they never get anywhere. Then they look at how far he went and they resent it.

"But no matter how much they talk about him, if he invites them to play with him, they do it. Then their attitude changes. I've seen even musicians' musicians, guys who play very precisely, come away with an entirely different opinion of him after playing in his band.

"One of the big reasons for his success is that he associated himself with some of the greatest polka musicians ever. Johnny Pecon, for example, was an all-time great on the accordion – polkas or anything else. Anything he heard he could play back instantly. Nobody was even close to him. Musically, Yonkee is bland. He doesn't get anybody mad at him."

BILL BYKOWSKI, night club owner, Milwaukee – "I know Frank for years, and he kept saying he wanted to play at my place to prove he could put over polkas there. All we feature is popular music, but he insisted. So I let him play on a Monday night for a private party. When people on the street heard the music they wanted to come in. Pretty soon we couldn't squeeze in another person. We only have room for three musicians on our stage, but at one time Yonkee had eight people playing up there."

BILL SRNICK, Cleveland drummer – "I played a few times with Yankovic. The job I remember most was at the Million Dollar Ballroom in Milwaukee in the late 1940s. He needed a drummer for the job, so he asked me to come along. Al Naglitch and Johnny Pecon showed up under the weather and Yonkee got real mad and said he wasn't going to let them play. But Georgie Cook calmed him down and said he'd get them ready. He went around giving them a lot of coffee and by the time the dance was supposed to start they were okay. The hall was packed when we got there. They had seven thousand people. They mobbed us like we were the Beatles. It took us a half hour just to get to the stage. We all had to sign autographs, even me, and I wasn't even a regular member of the band. It was so crowded that people couldn't dance. They just stood there and listened to us. The owner of the ballroom, Georgie Devine, was really enjoying himself. He came up on the stage and kept giving me hot foots all night."

DICK SODJA, musician, Cleveland – "I made several records with Yankovic. He always treated me well, first class all the way. We recorded in Nashville, Chicago and New York. He's the one who made the whole polka scene click."

MARION BELLE, Cleveland musician – "When you're on the bandstand with Yankovic, you know things are different. You know you're not just with a run of the mill musician and you push harder. There's a feeling that there's someone of great importance around, like you're in a room with a president of a steel company. He's a pro and he expects you to be a pro. He doesn't sympathize with you much. He'll give you one crack at a song and you better remember everything. Once we were playing the 'Secretary Polka,' in which the drummer has to make a sound like a typewriter. Our drummer couldn't get it and Yonkee swarmed all over him."

FRANK NOVAK, accordionist, Cleveland – "I hear the criticism about Frank. The musicians say anybody could have accomplished what Frank did. I always say to them, 'Well, why didn't you? You say you could have done it, but you didn't. Frank did.' "

CARL ROHWETTER, publisher, Michigan Polka News – "Yankovic is the man who Americanized polka music. He was the first to put English lyrics to significant polka or waltz music. He is the biggest man in the business."

AL TRATNIK, insurance agent, Milwaukee – "I'd never heard of Yonkee when they held the first polka contest. I stood in this big hall listening to all those great bands, Louie Bashell, Harold Loeffelmacher, and all the others. They were tremendous, wonderful. Then Yankovic came on and I thought this guy won't have a chance.

"When his band started playing, the sound came like a bang, like a shot out of a cannon. They completely overwhelmed the audience. As good as the others were,these guys were superior. It was no contest.

"Years later he was playing in Tahoe and I went to see him. I asked the parking lot attendant at the hotel where Yankovic was playing and he said, 'Who?' Then I asked the bellman where Yankovic was playing and he said, 'Who?' I began to think they had him hidden away in some little corner.

"Then I walked into the casino and I heard a voice calling over the microphone, 'Let's give a big hand to Al Tratnik from Milwaukee. Hello, Al.' It was Yonkee. He was playing on stage in the casino before a tremendous crowd, people standing all around.

"That was the time he celebrated his 25th wedding anniversary. He wanted June to come out, but she wouldn't. It hurt him. So we had a mock 25th wedding ceremony, with a woman from the audience filling in for June.

"Once I was at his steak house and my grandson, Doug, was with us. He was only four and he was getting sleepy, so we started to go. But Frank didn't want us to leave. He brought in two pillows and put Doug on them to sleep. Every once in a while he would dedicate a song to Doug, who was sound asleep. How many professional people would go to all that trouble?"

RON SLUGA, guitarist, Cleveland – "I still have hundreds of fan letters from the days when I played in Frank's band, from 1954 to 1956. I don't know why I still keep them, but I do. My kids get a charge out of reading them. The greatest thing about playing with him was that a lot of people lived to see him. He made a lot of people very happy. He was always pleasant to the people. I wish he was that pleasant to his musicians.

"Frank always paid well. We got even more than musicians in big bands got, but we'd have trouble occasionally. He fired me three times, you know. Then he'd call me back. It was never for musical things, but for personal reasons.

"He would get jealous if I got too much attention from the audience. I couldn't really blame him. It was his band, not mine. He even stranded me a few times on the road. He'd leave me somewhere and I'd have to catch a bus to get back with him.

"I had my honeymoon when I was on the road with him. I was only about 20 when I got married and my wife traveled with us for three months. We would drive together in my car and follow Frank's car. Sometimes he would try to lose us. That's Frank.

"But don't get me wrong. On the whole, I enjoyed working for him. I learned a lot from him. When I entertain I barely take a break, because that's the way Frank taught me. We were good friends. My wife babysat for his kids and his daughter, Linda, was in my wedding party. Frank and Kenny Bass played for my wedding."

HANS AMMELOUNX, restaurant proprietor, Milwaukee – "I put on Oktoberfests. I started with Mr. Yankovic and I'll stay with him all the way. He saved me last year when I put on a Springfest. The first night I had another band, a very good one, and nobody came. I took a beating. The next night Mr. Yankovic played and 5,000 people came through a storm to see him."

WALTER OSTANEK, Canada's Polka King – "Frank's one of a kind, even at his age. He doesn't know when to stop. He's always promoting. He has more spunk than a lot of 20-year-olds. I know when I'm with him there comes a time when I have to stop, but he keeps going. He is continuously working.

"Once I was with him at his house and he said, 'C'mon, let's go relax by the pool.' Five minutes later he had me helping him cover the pool for the winter.

"All kinds of things go into making him a success. For instance, he's willing to take a gamble. He takes jobs that others wouldn't risk. He was playing in Hawaii on a Saturday and he got an offer to play in New York on a Sunday. I wouldn't have taken the job for fear I couldn't get there in time. But he took it and was a big hit. He's unpredictable. Don't underestimate his playing. When the chips are down he can do anything with that box. If he had to play by himself, he'd put the job across.

"The amazing thing is that he has to work twice as hard because he uses so many different musicians. I know how tough it is to replace one man in a band. He constantly uses entire new bands. He sacrificed his life for polkas."

ED CHAY, travel agent, Chicago – "Yankovic loves people. Some entertainers take people on a trip and they demand the best of everything for themselves. They want the best suites and best accommodations. Frank has never said anything like that. He says, 'I want to be with the people. Give me the same kind of rooms as they have.' "

TOPS CARDONE, accordionist, Cleveland – "I really enjoyed my time with the Yankovic band. I made a lot of friends on the road and I still hear from them. This year alone at least 15 people from those days visited me or called me when they were in Cleveland."

JEAN JELENC, funeral director, Milwaukee – "Frank has had so much trouble in his life I'm surprised he still has the heart to sing. I was at his daughter Linda's wedding. He had just gotten out of the hospital after his car wreck and people were saying he'd never walk again. When he walked Linda down the aisle, I cried. He was the first man to sing songs in Slovenian on network television when everybody else was ashamed to."

DENNY BONECK, musician, Chicago – "I went to Alaska with Frank. We played in Fairbanks when the temperature was 46 below zero. People just wanted to touch us. They said they'd heard of us, but this was the first time they had a chance to see us. Frank is more than just my boss. He's a close friend. I hope he lasts until he's 150."

RICHIE VADNAL, bandleader, Cleveland – "I played with Yonkee one summer when I was just out of high school. On my first job we played in a little town in Pennsylvania and we stayed in a rinky-dink hotel. Abe Lincoln must have slept there. Yonkee told me to sleep upstairs with the banjo player, Eddie Teener.

"We were in the bar having a few drinks and Teener said he was going to turn in. He was a slim, good-looking guy. I'd never seen him before. After about an hour I went upstairs too and went into our room and I saw this bald-headed old fellow in there, toothless and paunchy. I thought I was in the wrong room and started out. But it was Teener, without his toupee and false teeth. He said, 'Hey, kid, where you going?'

"Just today I was driving home and I was thinking about Yonkee and all the musicians he's gone through. He was playing long before I came along and a lot of guys who were my age have already retired, but he's still going.

"When I was with him, Ron Sluga and I traveled in our own car and we'd leave Pittsburgh and Yonkee would say, 'I'll see you in Chicago,' and take off. We couldn't keep up with him. I remember we always had a lot of blowouts.

"When you played for him you knew you were working for a perfectionist. He wanted the microphone cords set just so on the floor and he'd like to play perfectly clean on the start and finish of each song. In between anything went.

"No doubt about it, he's the No. 1 man in polkas. He kept 'em going."

LAURA GLOZR, fan, Cicero, Illinois – "My husband and I hired Frank to play at our 25th wedding anniversary party. I only wanted a small party, but when the word got out that he was playing, everybody and his brother began calling me, asking for invitations. I could have had 5,000 people at the party, but when the list reached 500, I cut it off."

DICK KOSSINS, night club owner, Milwaukee – "Frank can come in from Cleveland with only his accordion and his amplifier, pick up four guys in town, and get away with it. People will sit around the stage with their mouths open and just look at him and never even notice the other guys. Nobody else can do that. He has the personality and the finesse."

EDDIE ARENZ, disc jockey, La Grange, Illinois – "Yankovic has a great memory for names. He met my wife and then he didn't see her again for eight years and he walked up to her and said, 'Hi, Nancy.' First time I ever heard him play was when I was in St. Cloud, Minnesota, with the national guard. My general said to me, 'I'm giving you the day off. You're driving me to see Yankovic.'

"We had Frank in Westmont, Illinois, to play for our Bicentennial celebration. It was amazing. We just put out the word that Frank was going to play and right away the whole town was talking about it."

LOU TREBAR, accordionist, Cleveland – "Yonkee has foresight and a good business head. He saw the potential of polka records before anyone else. He is a remarkable man."

LEE BOWER, ballroom operator, Sturtevant, Wisconsin – "The first time I booked Frank the music was supposed to start at 9:30 and the place was filled at 7:30. He's the granddaddy of them all. Everyone looks up to him."

EDDIE BUCAR, disc jockey, Willoughby, Ohio – "I take my hat off to Yankovic. He started this whole ball of wax. People don't realize how often he's given his time and played for free either. Many a time I've seen him come into a Slovenian or Croatian hall and somebody will hand him a button box and he'll play for 45 minutes. That's the kind of guy he is.

"There are musicians who don't like him, but that's plain jealousy. All musicians are on pedestals. This accordion player thinks he's better than that accordion player. But all these guys who claim to be the best today should indirectly be thankful to Yankovic, because without him they might not have anyplace to play.

"My son Dennis has played the bass with Yonkee many times and he says, 'When you play with the King, you live like a king.' "

GRANT KOZERA, accordionist, Milwaukee – "When I was six years old I was playing the toy banjo and he had me come up on the stage. He told the audience my name and I played a few numbers with him. Only a great personality could have done that. After I saw him play, I began to take accordion lessons. I'm 17 now and he still calls me up to play with him."

BILL DUNLAVEY, retired saxophonist, Cleveland – "I haven't seen Frank in years. I can't go to those places anymore. One more drink and I'd be gone. The doctor told me. I played in Frank's bands 40 years ago. We got along all right. A lot of guys are jealous of him. Not me. More power to him. He had to work hard for what he got."

RAY SMOLIK, pianist, Cleveland – "I played with Yankovic about six years. We had a lot of arguments on the road. You know how it is. You're traveling and there's nothing to do, so you argue. It's almost like you're arguing to pass the time. He wasn't the easiest guy to work for. He always picked on the new guys. But he treated me well enough.

"I remember that bus he had. It was like a truck. Once he tried to drive it thtrough four feet of snow and it wouldn't move. So he just laughed and said, 'The hell with it.' We stayed there and had a good time on the bus.

"As a musician he is only average, but if I wanted to sell anything to anybody at any time I'd hire him. He could sell the Brooklyn Bridge. He is the best showman and persuader I ever saw."

BOBBY CHICK, drummer, Chicago – "Some bandleaders panic when their musicians start to retire. One key man hangs 'em up and the bandleader will start to fail right there. They get wrapped up in their musicians and feel they can't get along without them. Frank is different. He'll always have his audience, even when he's 80. I think he'll carry his accordion to the grave with him."

BILL SAVATSKI, accordionist, Pewaukee, Wisconsin – "Frank IS polka music in this country. He is the only American polka musician who ever hit the big time and probably nobody else will ever do it. Traveling bands are almost a thing of the past, but Frank is a musical institution. People will come out to see him on a Tuesday or Wednesday, where they couldn't be bothered with an average band.

"He's good to work for, if you do your job. He jumps on you if you don't. We were playing once before a small crowd and I was tired and I guess I wasn't trying too hard. He gave me hell. 'We give 'em the best we have, if there's one person here or 1,000,' he said."

BUDDY GRIEBEL, pianist, Cleveland – "It seemed like Frank lived his life on the stage. He jumped around and was always smiling. I felt Frank got rid of a lot of anger by driving fast and by driving the band so hard on the road. We'd drive all night and we'd get into a new town dead tired and he'd say, 'All right, you can only sleep two hours. We got a personal appearance at noon.'

"He was a paradox. At times you'd want to drop him in a snow bank, you'd hate him so much. At other times he was unbelievably generous. All in all, I liked him. He was my best man when I got married."

JOE KUMEL, drummer, Cleveland – "I played in Frank's band once for a Little League fund-raiser. He played for nothing and paid us out of his own pocket. When I was a teen-ager, we had a club, the Big Time Operators. He played for us for free so we could raise money. But don't get him mad at you. Once he got a speeding ticket in Illinois that he thought was unjustified. After he paid, he went back on the freeway and stood there for two hours, flagging down cars and warning them about the radar ahead."

MARTY (KING) KUKOVICH, bass player, Pittsburgh – "I wouldn't trade my experiences with him for all the money in the world. Every job is different. People come up to him all night long for autographs. In the last eight or ten years the young people seem to want him more.

"I don't know how he can keep going the way he does. He must have steel in him. Maybe it's the home-made soup that keeps him so tough. He loves it, and no matter what part of the U.S. we played in the ladies would always have some good chicken soup or beef soup waiting for him."

AL MARKIC, bandleader, Cleveland – "He's had a terrific impact on polkas. A lot of people don't have the guts to do what he did. It's a tough life, living out of a suitcase. Even going on the road for a weekend is tough, let alone for year after year."

JOE WHITE, banjo player, Cleveland – "A lot of guys can play Frank into the ground, but they can't entertain anybody. We were playing in Waukegan and a woman in the audience got so excited she ran up on the stage and grabbed Frank. Then she fainted. I guess it was because we played a song that meant a lot to her.

"You feel good playing in his band because the crowds are always big. In St. Louis one night it was so crowded that when we took our intermission I had to go outside to the motor home to sit down. There wasn't a seat to be found in the hall.

"The polka was almost a dirty word in America until Frank came along. Then Frank went on network TV and sang songs in Slovenian rather than butter up the bigwigs. That took guts.

"One day I saw a priest at a hall we were playing in and he asked me what it was like playing for Yankovic. I said to him, 'We both work for perfectionists. You work for God and I work for Yankovic.' "

JEFF WINARD, accordionist, Milwaukee – "We played once in Gilbert, Minnesota, and they canceled the high school graduation so everybody could come to our dance."

AL NAGLITCH, pianist, Cleveland – "I played in Yonkee's bands from 1932 to 1948. He was the best. Where would polkas be without him? He was always a good guy.

"I haven't seen him for maybe ten years, but I just wrote him a letter the other day. I watch him all the time on the Polka Varieties TV show, so I thought it would be a good idea if he could come here and play for us in the Lake County Home in Painesville, Ohio, where I'm living now. We have about 30 people here and they all said they'd like to see Frank play. I told him I'd like to sit in with him for old times sake. We have a brand new Hammond organ here."

DOC PERKO, tavern owner, Milwaukee – "I took him around to meet all the tavern people and disc jockies when he first came to Milwaukee. People asked me why I pushed him over our local bands and I said, 'This guy has something extra. Some day everybody will know he's the champ.' I was right."

KEN NOVAK, musician, Cleveland – "Yankovic shouldn't be judged as a musician, but as a super entertainer, one of the few in polkas. You shouldn't just listen to him play. You have to watch the whole picture of his performance and the effect he has on the crowd. When he's up there, he owns a room for three hours. Nobody can turn on people the way he does.

"I'm a graduate of the Cleveland Institute of Music and I probably work more jobs than any musician in town, about 400 a year. As a professional, I follow his philosophy. I play for the people, not to impress other musicians, just like he does. The public doesn't care if you have a fancy arrangement. Simplicity is the secret to his success.

"Yonkee is big enough to make jokes about. I imitate him and do a little comedy routine about him myself. If he wasn't big, what would be the use. If I imitate Joe Frshmaga, who's going to know who I'm talking about. Nobody else sounds like Yonkee.

"Tavern owners love him. They're only interested in what you can do for them financially. Once when I worked a tavern I asked the owner if he liked my music. He said, 'I'll let you know when I count the money at the end of the night.' That's why they like Yonkee. Who else can fill a place in Cleveland on a Wednesday night?"

JOEY MISKULIN, accordionist, Cleveland – "Frank always taught me not to let personal problems interfere with business. He said it was our duty to entertain people, no matter how bad we might be feeling. He said people don't care about our troubles.

"When his mother died we were playing in Tahoe and Frank flew home for the funeral. When he came back he said to us on the bandstand, 'I'm going to dedicate our first song to my mother. But this is just between us. I'm not going to mention it to the audience.'

"So we played 'The Beautiful Rose Waltz' in his mother's memory. He had a big smile on his face as he sang it, but tears were coming down his face."

ROBERT DOLGAN, writer, Cleveland – Like many people who have risen to the top of a profession, Yankovic has his enemies. I tried to get some of them to talk for publication, but they refused to do so. My suggestion to them would be that from here on they hold their peace. They had their opportunity to come into the open.

Readers who know Yankovic well may be disappointed that we haven't included one of his trademarks, his frequent use of the phrase, 'Bemti Boga,' in the book. That is a choice bit of Slovenian profanity. Yonkee didn't want it in, for fear it would offend some readers. He insists on wholesome entertainment, a characteristic of all performers who have lasted a long time.

Frantic Frank is a full, complex man. Even in his seventh decade, his appetites remain gargantuan. Lesser men would have been satisfied with much less, or become jaded, years ago. I didn't know Yonkee when he was 20, or even 40. He must have been a tiger.

Working with him on the book was a pleasure. He'd bring

out the sparkling burgundy and talk for hours. He never broke an appointment or got testy over tough questions. "Don't be afraid to ask me about anything you've heard about me," he said. "The more we tell, the more people will like it."

Once we finished working late at night and he got into his motor home alone and started driving toward Chicago where he was playing the next night. He got tired about 6 a.m., pulled into a gas station, and slept for four hours. Then he awoke refreshed and finished the trip.

There is tragedy in Yankovic's life, of course. Some people feel sorry for him because of the hectic pace he maintains. He seems to be a prisoner of his long love affair with the public. But nobody ever wrote a book about a guy because he was a good family man.

Watch Yankovic on stage and you can understand why he puts up with the furor of his life. For four hours he is totally happy. He looks amazingly young. When he comes home from a long, gruelling trip his side men may look weary, but he appears rejuvenated.

My guess is that whenever he plays for a polka crowd he is returning to the days of his happy youth. He is playing again for the boarders or for the gang at the Wrong Club, over and over and over. I think that deep down he feels that that culture was superior to what most Americans have today.

I am not among those who feel that Yankovic's accordion playing leaves much to be desired. I watched him on several occasions during the writing of this book, and all I know is I enjoyed myself thoroughly.

I hope that when his time comes he goes charging into the final arpeggio with a song and a whoop and a holler. Long live the King!